Samurai from Outer Space

Understanding Japanese Animation

Antonia Levi

Open Court
Chicago and La Salle, Illinois

**To order books from Open Court,
call toll free 1-800-815-2280.**

Open Court Publishing Company is a division of Carus Publishing Company.

Copyright © 1996 by Carus Publishing Company.

First printing 1996
Second printing 1997
Third printing 1998
Fourth printing 1999
Fifth printing 2000

Printed and bound in the United States of America.

Library of Congress Cataloging-in-Publication Data

Levi, Antonia, 1947–
    Samurai from outer space: understanding Japanese animation /
Antonia Levi.
        p.   cm.
    Includes bibliographical references and index.
    ISBN 0-8126-9332-9 (pbk. : alk. paper)
    1. Animated films—Japan.   I. Title.
NC1766.J3L48   1996   96-42186
791.43'3—dc20   CIP

Contents

Contents

Illustrations

"Cartoons?" they say. "Yes," I say. "Japanese cartoons?" they say. "Yes," I say. Then I tie them to a chair and put in the tape.

This book represents an even more shameless attempt to introduce Americans to the amazing world of Japanese animation. For those who are already hooked, it's also a great way to persuade parents, friends, and other critics that being a couch potato is really an exercise in inter-cultural communication. The best part of this argument is that it's perfectly true.

It's simply not possible to watch *anime* (Japanese animation) without picking up a smattering of knowledge about Japanese customs and beliefs. Most fans go far beyond a smattering. I hope that this book will take them further still into the roots of Japanese culture, into the myths, legends, and basic moral assumptions that underlie *anime* and make it so distinctive.

To do that, I have found it necessary to discuss many *anime* in considerable detail. Since one prized feature of *anime* is its unpredictability, I have tried not to reveal endings or other unexpected shifts in plot. Sometimes, however, there is no alternative. There are some spoilers in this book. *Makoto ni mōshiwake ga arimasen.*[1]

> [1] "I'm very, very, very sorry."

Having said that, let me also say that no knowledge of Japanese is required to read this book. Japanese words that are commonly used are explained in the text and in the glossary at the back of the book. All *anime* and *manga* (comic books) discussed in this book have been translated into English in some way at some time. A few may be out of print, however.

Because most translations render Japanese names in Western order with the personal name first and the family name following, I have stuck to that format in the interest of clarity. Readers should know, however, that the correct Japanese order is the opposite. In Japan, the all-important family name comes first, followed by the less important personal name. For example, Akane Tendo of ***Ranma ¹/₂*** should properly be styled Tendo Akane, Tendo-san, or possibly, Ms. Tendo.

Preface

Anime uses a wide variety of romanization systems. I have not changed the romanization of words and names used in titles, but all other Japanese words are romanized according to the standard Hepburn system. A macron over a vowel means that the vowel is long. The sound remains unchanged, the macron simply lengthens it.

I cannot begin to list all the people whose help made this book possible. For one thing, that list would have to include every student I have ever taught, and I have been teaching Japanese history for fifteen years. The list would also have to list all my own teachers, my colleagues, and everyone else with whom I ever discussed Japanese culture. It would also have to include my long suffering father and the many friends who put up with my erratic schedule and bad moods throughout the process of writing. More specifically, I owe my gratitude to my Stanford *sensei*, Peter Duus, and my two *sempai*, David Groth and Martha Tocco, for their unwavering support. Special thanks are also due to Jonathan Walters for his help in hunting down the Hindu origins of Japanese gods, and to Dan Kent for setting me straight on all matters relating to Osamu Tezuka. And I owe an enormous debt of thanks to MyPhuong Le, and the other members of the Manga Madness Animation Club for sharing their insights, questions, and above all, their tapes.

All errors, opinions, and outrageous assertions are my own responsibility.

Chapter One

The Birth of the American Otaku

Generation X calls it *anime* (pronounced AH-nee-may). The name itself is resonant with all the multicultural baggage this new generation of twenty-somethings seems destined to carry through their lives. The Japanese took the word from the French to describe all animated films. Then, the Americans took it from the Japanese to describe the unique type of animation that comes from Japan.

And keeps on coming. What this flood of dubbed and subtitled video cassettes really represents is a cultural exchange so ambitious that neither the Japanese nor the American government would ever have dared to plan it. The new generations of both Japan and America are sharing their youth, and in the long run, their future. However much their governments may argue about trade and security in the

Pacific, America's Generation X and Japan's *shin jinrui*[1] will never again be complete strangers to one another. The connection is not only with Japan. *Anime* has already spread across most of Asia. Future social historians may well conclude that the creation of the American *otaku* was the most significant event of the post–Cold War period.

To say that an *otaku* is an *anime* fan doesn't really describe the phenomenon. Like a lot of the concepts that find their way into America via *anime, otaku* is a word that completely defies translation. Technically, it is a formal usage of the Japanese word meaning "your." In Japanese slang, it refers to someone with an obsessive interest in something, a geek. One can be a computer *otaku,* a fashion *otaku,* or an *anime otaku.* In America, it refers exclusively to those who are obsessively interested in *anime.* In America, *otaku* are:

- people who will go without food to buy the latest video export from Japan,

- people who have erotic dreams about Yuri and Kei, two intergalactic troubleshooters collectively known as the "Dirty Pair,"

- people who attend *anime* conventions dressed only in an itsy-bitsy, teeny-weeny, yellow tiger-striped bikini like that worn by Lum in **Urusei Yatsura.**

- people who will, without provocation, tie their friends to chairs and force them to watch *anime* until they too are hopelessly addicted.

Some go even further, voluntarily spending hours in language labs learning the basics of a language that is far more difficult to learn than Spanish or German, namely Japanese. In Japan, calling someone an *otaku* is a good way to start a fight. In America, however, the term is rapidly losing all pejorative connotations and may actually represent a source of pride.

How many *otaku*[2] are there in America? It's hard to say, especially since many *anime* fans prefer to remain in the closet, too embarrassed at age twenty to admit a liking for cartoons. They needn't worry. *Anime*'s popularity is spreading quickly and being an *otaku* is fast becoming respectable. Translation services and distribution of dubbed or subtitled *anime* are big business with more companies entering the market regularly. National video franchises like Blockbuster Video devote an entire section to *anime* even in small rural towns, and the number of their offerings is growing fast. More than a dozen nation-wide, annual conventions offer *otaku* a chance to sample the newest and the strangest. Most *otaku* are also avid readers of *manga*, the seri-alized comic books on which most *anime* are based. The demand for English translations of *manga* is growing at an equally phenomenal rate. A variety of magazines from the scholarly *Mangajin* to the cheer-fully commercial *Animerica* cater to an *otaku* market. Almost every col-lege campus has at least a small *anime* club. Over four hundred of them maintain elaborate home pages on the World Wide Web. The chatter on the *anime* newsgroup (rec.arts.anime) is copious and increasing in scope as well as intensity. Americans still form the largest group of non-Asian *otaku*, but slowly European, Australian, and even some African and Middle Eastern voices are joining in.

Anime's popularity with young Americans is probably one of the biggest surprises of the nineties. For all the complaints about Genera-tion X's "sound byte mentality," and all the cracks about the "dumbing of America," this generation has chosen a form of entertainment that is uniquely difficult to appreciate. It's not just the language barrier. Subtitles and dubbing take care of that. Culturally too, *anime* comes without an operator's manual.

Anime author-artists tend to assume that they are creating for the Japanese domestic market exclusively. The fact that their product is now being seen by non-Japanese comes as a surprise and sometimes a source of confusion. Rumiko Takahashi, Japan's First Lady of *anime*, expressed it best in a 1989 interview with *Amazing Heroes*. When informed of the phenomenal popularity of her translated *manga* in the United States, she replied:

> If it's true, then I'm truly happy. But I must confess to being rather puz-zled as to why my work should be so well received. It's my intention to be putting in a lot of Japanese references, Japanese lifestyle and feel-ings . . . I really have to wonder if foreign readers can understand all this, and if so, how?

Ms. Takahashi's point is well taken. The truth is, many *anime* fans enjoy the product without worrying about its Japanese nature. There's nothing wrong with that. One of the things that makes art such an excellent medium for intercultural exchange is the fact that it allows for individual interpretations beyond what the artist intended. Still, watching *anime* without noticing that it's Japanese is a waste of a painless and useful learning opportunity.

Of course, how much you can expect to learn about Japan from *anime* depends a lot on how the product is marketed. Some distributors like AnimEigo take cultural exchange very seriously. Even a lighthearted comedy like ***Oh, My Goddess!*** comes with a written insert explaining cultural and translation difficulties, and the subtitles themselves include short footnotes regarding terms that defy translation. Another distributor, Pioneer, often includes a short explanation of relevant Japanese terms and customs in a separate video section following the *anime.* Streamline Pictures and Viz Video, on the other hand, provide such excellent dubbing that the viewer forgets the characters ever spoke anything but English. That has its virtues, but the Japanese flavor of the original is often completely lost.

What difference does it make? To answer that question, it's necessary to look at a specific case. For example, the *sempai-kōhai,* or upper classman–lower classman, relationship is a uniquely Japanese institution, very different from the relationship between a senior and a junior in the American school system. The *sempai* (upper classman) has considerable power over his/her *kōhai* and is entitled to respect regardless of his/her personal merits. The *sempai-kōhai* relationship is clearly depicted in three *anime:* ***Oh, My Goddess!***, ***The Crystal Triangle***, and ***Ranma ¹/₂.*** However, the differing translation methods determine how clearly this is understood by the viewer.

In ***Oh, My Goddess!***, college freshman Keiichi Morisato's life is rendered miserable by hordes of loutish, bullying *sempai.* Given Keiichi's small stature and the fact that his *sempai* are all huge hulks, their control over him could easily be misinterpreted as the result of a purely physical threat. AnimEigo doesn't let that happen. Even in the subtitles, the term, *sempai*, is not translated and an explanation of its meaning is added both in the video and in the written insert.

A similar relationship exists between Mina and Isao, the two graduate students who assist their archeology professor in searching for god's final message in ***The Crystal Triangle***, distributed with subtitles by U.S. Manga Corps. For those who understand Japanese, the relationship is clearly defined by the fact that Isao addresses Mina as *sempai.* In the subtitles, however, that form of address is simply changed to her personal name, and the Japanese-impaired are often puzzled by her assertive (or bossy, depending on your politics) behavior toward her male colleague. Failing to mention the *sempai-kōhai* relationship, does not affect the plot particularly, but it does disguise an interesting detail about gender relations in Japan: the fact that seniority and other forms of hierarchical ranking can often mitigate or even eliminate sexual inequalities.

The *sempai-kōhai* relationship also affects the behavior of Ranma Saotome and Tatewaki Kuno in **Ranma ¹/₂,** but that tends to get lost in Viz Video's dubbing. Thus, when Kuno tells Ranma "You will address me as upper classman Kuno!" early in their relationship, it simply sounds arrogant and unpleasant. That doesn't greatly affect the plot since Kuno actually is arrogant and unpleasant, but the way he insists on his *sempai* status also gives early warning of his tendency to hide his basic boorishness behind a mask of tradition. Nonetheless, he does have a right to demand that Ranma address him as *sempai*. By ignoring that right, Ranma reveals himself to be impudent and unconventional, and so gives ample warning of what to expect from him in the future. The English translation accurately conveys the main point: that these two are not going to get along. However it misses a lot of the more subtle hints regarding their respective personalities.

Impossible-to-translate-in-one-word concepts like the *sempai-kōhai* relationship often lead *otaku* to assume that subtitles are always more revealing than dubbed *anime*. Sometimes that's true, especially for *otaku* who have enough Japanese to make out at least some of the voice track, but a lot still depends on the distribution company. AnimEigo, originally known for its subtitles, now offers releases in both formats with the subtitles tailored toward the purists and the dubbed versions featuring a more colloquial style. Even so, the dubbed version of **Oh, My Goddess!** declined to translate *sempai-kōhai* into English and added an explanatory caption instead. On the other hand, A.D. Vision, which releases only subtitled *anime,* provides translations that convey overall meaning rather than a literal translation. Indeed, A.D. Vision's subtitles are sometimes funnier and racier than what is actually being said. Clearly, subtitles don't guarantee greater accuracy. Still, the presence of the original dialogue does prevent translations from going too far astray. That became evident when Viz Video, best known for its dubbing, released a subtitled version of **Ranma ¹/₂**. For the most part, the subtitles were identical to the script used for the dubbed version. In Viz Video's subtitles, as in the dub, *sempai* became "upperclassman." Kuno, however, ceased to misquote Shakespeare as he had in the dubbed version, and returned to misquoting Japanese warrior epics.

[3]Or *"boku?"* or *"atashi?"* or any other word meaning "me." The word used indicates the speaker's sex and social relationship to whoever he/she is speaking to. The nuances are complex, and *otaku* who are not thoroughly familiar with Japanese language and society are advised to stick to the most noncommittal form which is *"watakushi?"*

[4]Some enthusiastic *otaku* add their own subtitles to Japanese bought tapes, a practice known as "fansubbing. Fansubbing has led to some harsh words between them and *anime* distributors on the subject of copyright laws.

Most *otaku,* however, consider subtitled *anime* a "purer" form and claim to prefer them, although sales and rental statistics make that claim debatable. That's because there's a fair amount of language-related snobbery among *otaku.* This is apparent in the number of borrowed Japanese words and phrases that pepper their speech regardless of whether or not they actually speak Japanese. Miss Piggy may still think the chic response is "Moi?," but the true *otaku* knows that it is "Watakushi?"[3] The height of *otaku* status is achieved by obtaining new releases directly from Japan without subtitles or dubbing, and translating them for your friends.[4]

The dubbing versus subtitles controversy is one of the most hotly contested issues among *otaku.* Dubbing is winning. Both markets are growing, but the number of dubbing fans is larger than the number of subtitle fans. This is reflected in the prices. Really hard-core *otaku* remain loyal to their subtitles, but it costs them. Companies which produce both versions often charge as much as ten dollars more for subtitled editions than for dubbed ones. Subtitles are not more expensive to produce. Far from it. They cost less than dubbing which requires not only actors but some editing to make the words fit the mouth movements. Subtitles cost more because the market for them is so much smaller. Dubbing makes up for its greater costs in sheer quantity.

It's easy to sneer at dubbing, but the truth is that without it, the whole *anime* phenomenon would probably never have occurred. There is nothing new about dubbed *anime.* The first dubbed *anime* was Osamu Tezuka's **Tetsuwan Atomu** (the Mighty Atom) which appeared on American TV under the title **Astro Boy** in 1964. It had some success as a children's show. So did another Tezuka series, **Kimba the White Lion**, which aired in 1966. **Kimba** was not only dubbed, but was also changed from its Japanese style sequential form to the episodic approach common to children's cartoons in America. The fact that **Astro Boy** and **Kimba** were of Japanese origin was not considered to be a selling point, and many Americans who saw them remained ignorant of that detail. **Astro Boy** and **Kimba** had a modest success with American youngsters. Indeed, despite Disney Studio's vigorous denials, many American and Japanese *otaku* remain convinced that **Kimba** was an important influence (possibly subconscious) on the animation team that produced *The Lion King*.[5] However, **Astro Boy** and **Kimba** remained one-shot deals. A few other *anime* followed, but none achieved the success of **Astro Boy** and **Kimba**.

At least, that was true until the 1980s when **Space Cruiser Yamato** and **Macross** made their first appearance on American television. Retitled **Star Blazers** and **Robotech**, respectively, they were heavily edited to accommodate American tastes and sensitivities. The names of all main characters were changed to make them less foreign and easier to remember. Thus, Susumu Kodai became Derek Wildstar, Yuki Mori became Nova, Hikaru Ichijo became Rick Hunter, and Misa Hayase became Lisa Hayes. Some characters underwent more significant changes. Dr. Sado, the hard-drinking medical officer of the **Space Cruiser Yamato**, must have attended AA meetings before signing on as Dr. Sane of **Star Blazers**. Yellow Dancer, a campy transvestite who played a supporting role in the Japanese original, underwent an even more drastic transformation for **Robotech**. The censors cut as much as they could, and then rewrote the script to make him a secret agent. His periodic appearances in drag were thus explained as a disguise to allow him to infiltrate enemy lines as a female pop star. Why did he need to be a female pop star? Don't ask.

[5] In August, 1994, fifty Japanese animators and 150 other people associated with the *anime* industry sent a letter to Disney expressing their regret that Tezuka's influence had not been acknowledged. Disney's lawyers, apparently unable to grasp the fact that this was a question of courtesy rather than copyright infringement or punitive damages, responded defensively and with a level of legalistic arrogance unusual even for them.

In fact it's better not to ask too much about the plots of either **Star Blazers** or **Robotech**. Plot was never their strong point even in the Japanese originals. Basically, both concern alien invasions and Earth's response. In **Star Blazers**, Earth succeeds by rebuilding a sunken battleship, the *Yamato*, as a space ship. Its technology is impressive, but it is also the spirit of the original *Yamato* that makes the new spaceship so invincible. Unfortunately, the real *Yamato* was a World War II battleship, and its original spirit was to fight Americans. Needless to say, this point was not stressed on American TV, and so the whole issue of the ship's spirit was lost. **Robotech** suffered even more mutilations. In **Macross**, the alien invasion was stopped by the magical voice of a pop singer. American producers decided, probably correctly, that Americans wouldn't buy that, especially since they were unfamiliar with the Tokyo pop scene. Substituting a more conventional ending, however, meant dumping the series' sentimentally pacifist message. It also involved adding on edited portions from two other, unrelated *anime* series, **Genesis Climber Mospeada** and **Super-dimensional Cavalry Southern Cross**, making **Robotech** less a dubbed *anime* than a whole new creation.

There were other, more subtle, changes too. The long, drawn out stills used to convey moments of extreme emotion or heroism were shortened, and the sound track was changed. Flaws and contradictions in the heroes' personalities were softened. The deaths of some significant characters were covered up. And just to put the final kiss of death on the whole production, the networks persisted in scheduling them at times suitable for children. The distributors protested in vain that these cartoons were not for kids. Aside from the sex and violence, most of which ended up on the cutting room floor, they featured elaborate plot lines and character studies that most children would find hard to understand. Their protests were ignored. To the American television industry, if it was animated, it was kiddie fare.

In fact, it didn't matter. Teens tuned in anyway, even at 7:00 in the morning. They knew that what they were watching was different, special. When they grew older, they found out why it was different, where it came from, and they went looking for more. That, of course, was the beginning of *anime* in America. Well, one of the beginnings anyway.

Star Blazers and **Robotech** laid the base, but they did not do it alone. Two other factors ensured that these Japanese imports did not go the way of **Astro Boy** and **Kimba**: reasonably priced VCRs and increased Japan-America student exchange programs. American students went to Japan on exchange programs before the 1980s, of course. And most of them developed a taste for *manga* and *anime*. And when they got home, most of them tried to share their new discoveries with their American friends. The trouble was that they had nothing to show except for a few thick, black and white comics that opened the wrong way, and that no one else could read. Their repeated assertions that the Japanese were doing some really interesting things with animation fell on deaf ears. The number of exchange students who chose to go to Japan before the 1980s (I mean, what's wrong with Paris?) was small in any case.

All that changed in the 1980s. Alarmed by Japan's economic success, America boosted the number of exchange programs in the hope that the new students would learn Japan's secret, or at least return better equipped to deal with Japanese businessmen. Whether they did or not, most of that small army of exchange students returned with *anime*, this time on cassettes. This time, they had something to show. And this time, prepped by their exposure to **Star Blazers** and **Robotech**, their friends showed an interest.

So did the business world. Streamline Pictures (the dubbing specialists) was formed in 1988. AnimEigo (subtitles) and The Right Stuf (vintage *anime* and discounts) followed in 1989. U.S. Manga Corps hung out its shingle in 1991. Then came AD Vision, Pioneer, Central Park Media, Manga Entertainment, and Viz Video. *Anime* is here to stay.

It's probably just as well that *anime* didn't reach America until the 1980s. If it had come any earlier, it's doubtful that it would have been as popular as it now is. *Anime* has changed significantly in the past ten or fifteen years, and for the most part, it's changed for the better. Okay, Osamu Tezuka did some interesting things in the 1960s and early 1970s. He didn't just create **Astro Boy** and **Kimba the White Lion.** Tezuka was also the creator of **Princess Knight**, featuring the first of those cross-dressing, hard-fighting women so popular in *anime* today, **The Phoenix**, a story of reincarnation that began in Japan's mythological past and continued into the far future, and a huge variety of shorter experimental works. But as far as Japanese animation was concerned, Tezuka was pretty much it.

Manga, those black and white comic books on which most *anime* are based, were more pervasive of course, but even they were different. For one thing, they were strictly divided along gender lines. Boys' and men's *manga* (*shōnen manga*) were devoted to action. They focused on war, sports, sex, and sometimes business rivalries. Plots were strong, but character development was weak. Eyes were smaller, too. *Manga* artists use the eyes to indicate emotions and sensitivity, not a high priority in these early *shōnen manga.*

Girls' and women's *manga* (*shōjo manga*) were precisely the opposite. They focused on emotions and personal relationships. Plots were weak. Eyes, however, were enormous. Almost nothing happened, but you certainly knew exactly how everyone felt about whatever it was that wasn't happening.

Even if they had been available in English, Americans would probably have found both forms extreme. American men might have been intrigued by some of the male *manga*, especially the sexually explicit ones, but it's hard to imagine American women enjoying the sugary sweet romances of early *shōjo manga.*

Actually, Japanese women had some problems with that at first, too. The first *shōjo manga* weren't even written by women. They were written by men whose portrayals of what they imagined girls and women really thought and felt often missed the mark. Still, something was better than nothing, and Japanese girls bought whatever the distributors put out. *Shōjo manga* rapidly became a permanent feature on Japanese newsstands. Some of the girls who grew up reading them also grew up convinced they could do a better job.

They were right. They became Japan's first generation of female cartoonists. After a short scuffle in the 1960s, they took over the genre. And *shōjo manga* began to change in a way that would eventually change all *manga* and so, *anime*. Emotions and personal relationships were still important, but so were plots. Girls, like boys, wanted some action in their stories, and they wanted to see girls or women they could identify with involved in that action.

That posed a problem. The first generation of female *manga* author-artists were not feminists in any Western sense of the word or, if they were, they knew better than to say so. Obviously none of them were completely traditional either. If they had been, they would not have chosen a career, not in 1960s Japan. But, regardless of their personal views on women's rights, they had their readers' tastes to consider. Perhaps even more important, they had their readers' parents to consider.

As a result, the first wave of *shōjo manga* written by women for girls dealt with a never-never land called the West, preferably the historical West. In that never-never land, women were strong and ambitious. They still lived for romance, but they also led interesting and exciting lives. Often they masqueraded as men in order to do things that might seem otherwise impossible for women. Even the men they loved and often lost had a female look to them. They were pretty men with eyes as large and lustrous as any woman and sensitive, caring natures.

To some degree, these men are a universal adolescent female fantasy: romantic, communicative, and sexually nonthreatening. That's the easy, pop-psychology explanation, but as is often the case with things Japanese, the full reason is a bit more complex than that. What the men in these early *shōjo manga* really looked like were not just idealized males, but the male impersonators of the Takarazuka theater. The Takarazuka theater is an all-female troupe of a type unique to Japan. It caters almost exclusively to a teen-age female audience, and its stars are usually the male impersonators. Indeed, for many Japanese girls, their first experience of romance is a crush on one of these male impersonators. Japanese parents do not see these adolescent crushes as signs of lesbianism. It is considered a normal part of growing up, and many parents consider it nicer, "purer" if the first object of a young girl's affection is female rather than male. In fact, a close relationship developed between the Takarazuka theater and *shōjo manga*. In the 1960s and early 1970s when *anime* were far less common, popular *shōjo manga* were more likely to find dramatic form on the Takarazuka stage than in animation.

The two influenced each other and produced a new genre. The Takarazuka theater had always done some Western skits in which they used wigs and make-up to create Caucasian features. Now they did more, sometimes whole plays like the 1974 hit, **The Rose of Versailles**, based on a best-selling *manga* about an aristocratic swordswoman in revolutionary France. However, Takarazuka also had a long tradition of performing more conventional Japanese dramas in which Japanese women played unusually powerful roles, often by masquerading as men. They also specialized in portraying *bishōnen,* those beautiful androgynous young men whose courageous exploits and bisexual romances pervade Japan's traditional warrior legends.

That had an impact on *shōjo manga* which began to introduce more home-grown themes and heroines. Increasingly, *shōjo manga* began to resemble male *manga* in plots, although the central characters remained female. Japan itself became a never-never land in which the captain of the female high school volleyball team was as important and as admired as any boy. Female warriors rode to the rescue of the unfortunate, spaceships with all-female crews blasted off for the stars, and women in love pursued their men aggressively. *Manga* women sometimes still had to cross-dress in order to live this way, but at least they no longer had to be Western.

Their appearance, however, did not change, resulting in an aspect of *anime* that often baffles American audiences: the Caucasian features of unmistakably Japanese characters. Asking Japanese friends to explain this doesn't help. They are baffled by the question. To contemporary Japanese, the large, round eyes and varied hair colors of *anime* characters no longer indicate race. What began as a portrayal of Westerners, became a distinctive style in *shōjo manga*.

By the 1960s, the huge eyes were no longer so much a racial trait, as a gateway to the character's soul. Those eyes could glisten with hope, blur with tears, or melt with love. Sometimes they glistened a bit too much. Takahashi had a field day making fun of those eyes in the "Attack of the Girly-Eyes Measles" episode of **Urusei Yatsura**. Those eyes can also go dead in a thoroughly frightening fashion. This is the case in the final episode of **Iczer One** when Nagisa's mind is taken over by Iczer Two. Her eyes, normally moist and glistening, are reduced to matte-finished circles, devoid of life or thought. The same thing happens to Yohko Mano when she is almost seduced[6] by Osamu in the opening episode of **Devil Hunter Yohko**. Eyes, in short, are a way of indicating emotion, something that is not always easy to do with a black and white drawing, or even with the greater flexibility of animation. That has carried over into today's *anime* where sensitive, sympathetic characters usually have larger eyes than other characters. Women generally have larger eyes than men. But don't count on it absolutely. *Anime* artists have their individual styles and idiosyncrasies on this.

The different hair colors of *anime* characters also derive from early *shōjo manga*. Not only were early *shōjo manga* interested in portraying Westerners, they were also interested in portraying complex emotions. Panels tended to be ornate, featuring symbolic backgrounds and overlays. For example, an overlay of flowers might indicate love in bloom, while crashing waves superimposed on an embracing couple was a delicate suggestion of orgasm. Background tableaux often indicated a character's thoughts and memories. Overlays and odd juxtapositions of characters could also be used to convey their relationships to one another.

Because of the complexity of such panels, *shōjo manga* relied heavily on shading and contrast. To realistically portray all Japanese with dark hair was aesthetically awkward. As a result, the artists continued to portray one character with inked-in hair while another might have shaded locks or hair indicated only by line drawing. In the black and white pages of the *manga* this was obviously stylistic, but on the colored *manga* covers and later in the full-colored world of *anime*, that shading became blond, brunette, or red hair. Other colors are sometimes used too: purples, pinks, and greens, for example. Of course, these days, those hair colors can also be seen on the streets of Tokyo.

That's not to say that hair color is utterly without meaning. As might be expected in a country where most of the population has black hair, that color has positive connotations. Other shades are suspect until proven otherwise. Not all black-haired characters are perfect, but they are apt to be more sympathetic and more traditionally Japanese than those featuring other shades. In **Ranma ¹/₂**, a comedy series with a sex-changing hero, hair color is very important. As a boy, Ranma has thick black hair. When he changes into a girl, he becomes smaller, curvier, and acquires a truly enviable bust. He also becomes a redhead. That change in hair color not only helps differentiate the two personas, it is also a tip-off as to which is the real, the proper Ranma. Akane (Ranma's own true love although neither of them ever admit it) also has thick, black hair, indicating that despite her tomboyish, kung-fu fighting approach to love, she is fundamentally sound and sincere. Of course, Kodachi Kuno, the self-styled "Black Rose," also features long black hair, but hers is a bit too insistently black. In fact, her whole persona is too insistently that of a very proper, traditional Japanese miss. She is a walking satire. It's harder to explain why Ryōga, the eternally befuddled young man who turns into a piglet, and Mousse, the Chinese martial artist who turns into a duck, also have black hair. Both characters are undeniably strange and Mousse isn't even Japanese. The rules are not absolute, even in a single work of a single artist.

Watch out for blonds though! They're usually a sign of trouble if not actual evil. Rieg, the larcenous archeologist in **Explorer Woman Ray**, is typically tall, blond, and smooth-talking. Of course, he is also vaguely European. That's not the case with Asuka Ryō, the cold, ruthless young man who persuades his gentle, good-natured classmate (lots of black hair there!) to merge with a demon in **Devilman**. Asuka's blond hair combined with his many other eccentricities give credence to his own explanation that his nature is not pure enough to dominate in a case of demon possession. C-ko, whose non-existent charms cause so much rivalry in the **Project A-ko** series, is another blond we are asked to accept as a Japanese schoolgirl. (Of course, she may also be an extraterrestrial, but that transpires later.) C-ko isn't exactly evil. She just has a personality that's slightly more irritating than the screech of chalk on a blackboard. Blond hair can mean a lot of different things. The one thing it doesn't mean, however, is Caucasian.

When Caucasian characters are portrayed in *anime*, the artist may add some racial features such as freckles or a large, oddly shaped nose. In *manga*, Westerners often speak in *katakana*, a phonetic syllabary usually reserved for borrowed words. In *anime*, that sometimes becomes a distinctive accent. That feature, of course, is often completely lost in dubbing and requires a good ear for Japanese even when the original sound track is still present. Characters' names are also a tip-off, although names that sound Western to Japanese, Kiddy Phenil of **Silent Möbius** or Rieg of **Explorer Woman Ray**, for example, may simply sound odd to Westerners. The situation is further complicated by the fact that so many *anime* are science fiction, and will often deliberately combine a Japanese name with a non-Japanese identity (or vice versa) to indicate a future in which intercultural marriage is the norm. This is certainly the case in **Macross Plus** which features a multiracial, multi-special cast of characters with distinctive nasal appendages.

In fantasy or futuristic *anime*, race isn't usually an issue anyway. And even when it is, it's not likely to result in any major changes. Racism is certainly a problem for Nadia, the heroine of **Nadia: The Secret of Blue Water**, who makes her living as a circus performer in turn-of-the-century France. Nadia knows she is different, but due to memory problems, she isn't sure whether she comes from India or Africa. She is right to be confused. Her skin is a deep brown and she dresses exotically, but her features are exactly the same as those of the Europeans. Like most *anime* characters, Nadia doesn't really look like any race. Her face is an oval with big eyes, a quick hook for a nose, and a tiny mouth. It's a basic human face reduced to its minimum components. She's lucky. When Japanese animators try to portray Africans or Indians (or Arabs or Native Americans or anyone other than East Asians) realistically, the results are often grotesque stereotypes.

Gender stereotyping is also common, of course, but it's not as one-sided as Americans often assume it will be. Today's *anime* are seldom based on *manga* that can clearly be identified as either *shōjo* or *shōnen manga* in style. In order to appeal to as wide an audience as possible, *anime* producers favor *manga* that straddle the two worlds. There are more and more of them.

The range of *shōjo manga* increased steadily over the years. By the 1980s, the term *shōjo* (young girl) was no longer really appropriate. Some were still aimed at girls but, like their male counterparts, others were clearly designed for a more mature audience. They dealt with controversial issues like illegitimacy, incest, and abortion. Some focused exclusively on men and various aspects of male life, although the approach was still distinctively female, analytic, erotic, and interestingly enough, tinged with pity. A subcategory of *shōjo manga* called *bishōnen* (beautiful boy) *manga* developed which focused on gay male romance. Most Americans assume these are intended for a gay male audience, but they are not. They cater almost exclusively to heterosexual girls and women.

Increasingly, female animators have also begun to introduce themes which critique the existing state of male-female relations in Japan, and suggest that things might be otherwise. Rumiko Takahashi does this with humor in her popular series **Ranma ¹/₂**, in which a young man falls under a curse that causes him to change into a woman whenever he is splashed with cold water. Needless to say, he learns more about discrimination and unwanted male attentions than he ever wanted to know. A new four-woman group called CLAMP does it with sex in **RG Veda**, portraying heterosexual male characters as provocatively (or exploitatively, depending on how you feel about these things) as male artists portray *manga* women. Hagio Moto does it intellectually in **They Were 11**, a science fiction mystery in which an androgynous alien must choose whether to become male or female when it comes of age. It's not feminism in the Western sense, but it makes Japanese men nervous, and it should.

In the late 1970s and early 1980s, the gap between male and female *manga* began to close. By then, boys and men openly read and enjoyed *shōjo manga*, and vice versa. This trend directly contradicts the claims made by American network executives that they cannot produce childrens' shows with strong female leads because, although girls easily identify with male heroes, boys refuse to watch shows with a female star. Japanese boys, at any rate, have no such problem. And, judging from the early success of newly dubbed kiddie classics like **My Neighbor Totoro**, American boys don't really mind female heroes either, provided they are doing something a bit more interesting than sticking sequins in a plastic horse's mane.

In the 1980s, the styles of male and female *manga* also began to merge. Eyes got bigger in male *manga* and smaller in *shōjo manga*. Male *manga* began to feature stronger female characters with larger roles, occasionally even leading roles. *Shōjo manga* did the same and sometimes featured male heroes. By the middle of the 1980s, it was often difficult to tell one from the other except by noting which company had published it. Even knowing the sex of the author-artist no longer helped since they often crossed over into one another's fields.

The 1980s was also the era in which *anime* came into its own in Japan. The practice of turning a *manga* into an animated film was not new, but prior to the 1980s, animation was an expensive honor reserved for only a few, exceptionally popular *manga*. Heartened by the tremendous success of such *anime* as **Macross**, **Space Cruiser Yamato**, and **The Castle of Caliostro** on Japanese television in the 1970s, not to mention the reduced costs of computer animation techniques, Japanese studios and television networks began to release increasing numbers of animated features. TV series such as **Urusei Yatsura** (also known in America as **Those Obnoxious Aliens** or

Lum) and **Gundam** pulled high ratings and paved the way for further series. Movies and OVAs (Original Video Animation: *anime* made for and released directly into the cassette market) soon followed.

This was the *anime* that found such an appreciative audience in America. No wonder it's so hard to understand. Even its physical appearance requires a lengthy discussion of Japan's postwar popular media. To examine the source of its dramatic techniques, its themes, and its basic assumptions, requires a deeper knowledge of Japan's prehistory, its myths and legends, its religions, artistic traditions, and philosophies. That's a lot of baggage for a cartoon to carry, and if you prefer to just put in a tape and enjoy the result without bothering about it, no one will blame you.

If you want to go further, however, *anime* can show you a side of Japan few outsiders ever even know exists. Unlike much of Japanese literature and movies, *anime* is assumed to be for local consumption only. That's important, because most Japanese are highly sensitive to outside pressure. Authors who know their novels will soon appear in translation, or film producers who know their works will be judged at the Cannes Film Festival, often feel constrained by that knowledge. It's not just that they want to show their country and culture in a good light, they also feel an obligation to make it intelligible to a global audience. Not so *anime* author-artists. At least, not yet. They write for and about Japanese. As a result, their work offers a unique perspective, a peeping Tom glimpse into the Japanese psyche.

And what a marvelous place that turns out to be! Who would have guessed all that was going on behind those dull business suits and tightly wrapped kimonos! It's so easy to dismiss the Japanese as workaholics, economic animals, and uncreative imitators. It's easy to forget that they are the inheritors of an ancient culture drawn from East Asia, but nurtured in isolation to produce something that surprises (and sometimes appalls) even its immediate neighbors. It's easy, until you watch your first *anime* or read your first *manga*.

But be warned. What you learn about Japan through *anime* can be deceptive. This is not the way Japanese really live. This is the way they fantasize about living. These are their modern folk tales, their myths, their fables. This is not a peep into the conscious Japanese mind, but into the unconscious. It will tell you things about Japan that no Japanese will ever tell, partly because they're too embarrassed, but mostly because these are things they take so for granted that it doesn't occur to them to explain.

Anime can also offer insights into American culture. The Japanese aren't the only ones who take their own assumptions for granted. We do too, and the contrast offered by *anime* can show us ourselves in a whole new light. For example, most Americans would agree that their culture is dominated by a Judeo-Christian tradition. However, few of them question the effect that has on them beyond a few details regarding religious practice and perhaps the Constitution. In fact, that tradition affects virtually every aspect of our lives. Regardless of whether we are religious or even believe in god, most of us have a monotheistic outlook. We believe in one answer, one way, one Truth with a capital T. And we believe in a universe that is, or should be, rational and just. We believe that virtue should be rewarded. We regard reason as more reliable than intuition. We believe that there is a sharp dividing line between reality and fantasy, between dreams and waking. We don't think about these things.

At least, we don't think about them until we find ourselves faced with something that clearly doesn't take those ideas for granted. *Anime* is one of those things. It comes from Japan and Japan is not a Judeo-Christian culture. Not in the least. And that means that the Japanese view of truth, the universe, reason, and reality are all very different. American *otaku* often say that *anime*'s charm lies in its unpredictability, its off-beat weirdness that makes you stop and think about things you never even noticed before. In fact, *anime* is more creative for Americans than it is for Japanese. It's a chance to see the world through a stranger's eyes, and that's a view that ensures we'll never look at ourselves quite the same way again.

Chapter Two

Disney in a Kimono

The Japanese have a disconcerting habit of comparing their own celebrities to Western counterparts. For example, the seventeenth-century Kabuki playwright, Monzaemon Chikamatsu, is often described as "the Shakespeare of Japan." Popular mystery novelist Masako Togawa becomes "the Agatha Christie of Japan." Film director Akira Kurosawa is "the Ingmar Bergman of Japan." And, not surprisingly, Osamu Tezuka is often referred to as "the Walt Disney of Japan."

But, like the other three examples, this description obscures more than it reveals. Tezuka certainly was the father of *anime* in the same way that Disney was the father of the American animation scene, but that's where the comparison stops. Tezuka freely acknowledged his debt to American animators, and was perfectly capable of imitating

Disney's style on occasion. In **Legend of the Forest**, an experimental film with an environmental message, he both acknowledged that debt and revealed how far he had gone beyond his early imitation of American animation. Tezuka's own style was quite different, both in its look and content. Tezuka, a medical doctor turned cartoonist, dominated the media in Japan from the 1950s through the early 1970s with long-running series such as **Astro Boy**, **Princess Knight**, **Black Jack**, **The Buddha**, and **The Phoenix**. Featuring elaborate plots and subplots with occasional religious and philosophical messages tossed in, Tezuka's work forced Japan to take *manga* seriously as a literary form.

Tezuka was also responsible for many of the first *anime*. Not only did he train many of the next generation of animators, he also founded his own studio. Frustrated by the hesitancy of the major studios, he founded Mushi Productions in 1962 to make and distribute animated versions of his own work. Unfortunately, business acumen turned out to be another trait Tezuka did not share with Uncle Walt, and Mushi Productions went bankrupt in 1973. But by that time, it had already set the pattern. *Anime* had come into its own as a unique form of theater which drew on all of Japan's historical, religious, and artistic traditions to create something uniquely suited to expressing the mood of late twentieth-century Japan. And, to judge from the way it's spreading, the late twentieth century anywhere.

What is it that American *otaku* find so attractive in this art form that was never intended for them? The answers are as individual as the *otaku* themselves, and that can be very individual indeed. But there are some points of agreement, some features of *anime* that most *otaku* will include in their list of what it is that makes *anime* so irresistible. It's a list that says as much about their own concerns as it does about *anime*. Briefly stated, these features are:

- the high tech look,
- the creative fantasy worlds,
- the genuine tension created by the fact that bad things happen to good people,
- the multidimensional characters,
- the robots, powersuits, and other *mecha*,
- the sexy, powerful women.

When *otaku* speak of the high tech look of *anime*, they usually compare it disparagingly with Disney. If only technology is considered, that's unfair. Disney Studio's productions are technologically far more sophisticated with their high cel count and smoothly flowing, realistic animation. *Anime*, by contrast, uses a low cel count which results in jerky, unrealistic movements. Backgrounds tend to be static and scenes are often linked together with stills in which nothing moves. What *otaku* are really talking about when they praise the high tech look of *anime* is the fact that Japanese animators are getting powerful dramatic effects with only a fraction of the financial and technological effort.

To some degree, this is a matter of necessity. *Anime* studios simply do not have the kind of budgets Disney animators take for granted. However, it is also a matter of choice. Unlike the West, Japan's artistic and theatrical traditions have never aimed at realism. Instead, both in art and drama, the Japanese have emphasized techniques that capture the essence of the subject in a way that assumes some participation by the audience. *Anime* sets the stage, but the viewer's imagination must fill in the gaps. *Anime*'s most powerful scenes never appear on the screen at all.

Such interactive art is a longstanding tradition in Japan. Japanese artists, particularly the woodblock printers of the sixteenth to nineteenth centuries whose influence on *anime* is as clear as the picture on the screen, specialized in deceiving their viewers into believing they had seen more than they had. Unlike the carefully limited and framed art of the West, woodblock artists delighted in subject matter that refused to be confined to the space available. A picture of flying kites, for example, includes some strings without a visible kite, leaving the viewer to fill in the fact that there are many more kites than those shown by the artist. In other woodblock prints, bridges and paths wander off into unseen territories, a single, powerful wave hints at the vast ocean behind it, and a crowded street scene suggests an urban vitality far beyond the few figures shown.

Woodblock prints also seem more realistic than they are. This is because the artists strategically apply detailing and elaborate shading in areas where they know the eye will focus, thus deceiving their viewers into assuming that everything in the picture is equally meticulous. It isn't. And it isn't in *anime* either. In fact, *anime*, with its bright, primary colors (although not quite the same primary colors American studios use) and *trompe l'oeuil* special effects, is really an extension of the traditional art of woodblock printing. Only now, this traditional Japanese art form moves, talks, and sings.

That makes it a form of theater. And there too, *anime* artists have drawn on their own heritage. From the all-male Noh and Kabuki theaters and the Bunraku puppet theater, they took and adapted a wide range of stylized actions and theatrical conventions. In particular, the use of heroic poses and tableaux to highlight dramatic moments made their way into *anime* in the form of stills. From the strolling *kami-shibai* storytellers who entertained village children with stories and pictures in the days before television, *anime* took its effective use of a narrative voice-over and its ability to present old tales in modern dress. From the all-female Takarazuka theater, *anime* took its stock of idealized male and female forms, as well as its unabashed sentimentality and sense of melodrama.

From all these sources, *anime* artists created a new art form. Of course, the new form retains characteristics of the old. This is true of nearly everything in Japan, but it is most evident in *anime* and in the popular media generally. In particular, Japan's popular media have retained that preference for the unreal over the real that characterized Noh, Kabuki, Bunraku, and the Takarazuka theater. When Americans are first exposed to Japanese video productions, animated or live-action, they are often critical of what they consider to be stagy backgrounds, contrived costuming, hammy acting, and unrealistic special effects. Later, they get used to it.

Actually, what they get used to is a whole different way of responding to dramatic entertainment. The effect of that contrived unreality is to create a different kind of empathic response in the audience, one that does not necessarily disengage the mind. Traditional Western drama tries to enfold the audience utterly, to persuade the audience that what they see is really happening. Ideally, the empathy created between viewer and production is so complete that the difference between reality and fiction is temporarily lost. Japanese drama, on the other hand, goes out of its way to remind the audience during the course of the production, that what they are seeing is unreal. Bertolt Brecht, a German playwright of the 1920s who was strongly influenced by Asian theatrical techniques, called this effect "aesthetic distance." He argued that by insisting on the fictional nature of the experience, Asian drama allowed the audience to think more fully about what they were seeing.

"Aesthetic distance" doesn't mean that there is no empathic response to Japanese drama. No one who has ever watched a Japanese family gather before their TV with a full box of tissues in order to watch their favorite soap opera could doubt that empathic response is both desired and experienced on such occasions. What it does mean, however, is that Japanese seldom confuse their own life experiences with those they have experienced through fiction. This may help to explain why, despite the extraordinary amount of violence on Japanese television, the nation as a whole remains relatively peaceful and crime free.

The popularity of *anime* among young Americans suggests that they, too, are tired of having their emotions raked so ferociously and realistically across the coals on a nightly basis. In *anime* they have found a form of entertainment that satisfies their highly nurtured taste for action, suspense, and visual stimulation without leaving them drained of all feeling and thought. Young America's growing taste for *anime* is as telling a criticism of American television as their desire to turn off the TV set.

"Aesthetic distance" is a Western theory. To the Japanese, that's just the way drama is, although it may explain why popular American shows so often do poorly in Japan. The Japanese have their own explanation for this preference for the unreal in drama. They argue that the unreal can capture the essence of reality better than reality itself because it is universal rather than individual. Thus, a Kabuki female impersonator embodies the essence of femininity better than any real woman, a Takarazuka male impersonator does the same for masculinity, and the Bunraku puppets (or animated drawings) represent humanity better than any human actor. Or at least, that's the theory. This has led some Westerners to conclude that the Japanese prefer artificiality. That's true, but it is also over-simplistic. Actually, what they prefer is symbolism.

The use of a single, small symbol to express a greater, universal whole is basic to most traditional Japanese arts. The Japanese garden, for example, may use a few rocks and some raked sand to create an image of islands in a vast sea. Flowers, symbolically arranged, can embody elaborate philosophical ideas about the relationship of humanity to Heaven and Earth. The Tea Ceremony creates a symbolic social order within an enclosed space. *Haiku* poetry uses seventeen carefully chosen syllables to evoke complex imagery and emotions. And traditional woodblock printing uses a small, detailed scene to suggest the larger scene that surrounds it.

Anime, too, uses symbols to convey both content and mood. In this respect, *anime* is more of a challenge for Americans than for Japanese. That's not necessarily because they are lazier or less imaginative than the Japanese. Americans often miss the more obvious symbols embodied in *anime* simply because they are unfamiliar with the visual cues. *Anime* has its own traditions, many of which make little sense to a newcomer. For example, how is any American supposed to guess that when a male character has a nose bleed, it indicates sexual arousal? Or that if the blood explodes in all directions, it means an ejaculation? Or that when the camera zeroes in on a character or pulls back in a long still, it means that what follows is a flashback? Sometimes there is no indication at all. **Silent Möbius**, a science fiction *anime* in which the plot relies on several explanatory flashbacks, has been confusing American viewers for years with this little trick.

Other clues are lost or even misinterpreted because of differing cultural assumptions. Seasonal change, for example, has great meaning for the Japanese, so much so that even network news in Japan features a daily segment on what's blooming or changing color or just dropping from the sky. Most *anime* includes some indication of the season early on, thereby offering a subtle hint of what is to follow. Americans can recognize the seasons as a rule, but their interpretations may be way off. In **Doomed Megalopolis**, for example, an old cherry tree sheds its delicate blossoms as the priestess Keiko leaves her shrine to face down demons in 1920s Tokyo. Most Americans simply register the fact that it's spring. Others may go further assuming that it means Keiko will soon be deflowered (true), or that she is destined for a time of hope and renewal (not true). To the Japanese, cherry blossoms are also associated with death, and with an aesthetic concept known as *mono no aware*.[1] This is the idea that nothing is quite so beautiful as something which is about to end. Its very impermanence adds to its beauty. Cherry blossoms are considered particularly lovely because their duration is so short. Samurai were often compared to cherry blossoms as they rode off to battle. The *kamikaze* pilots of World War II were likened to falling cherry blossoms as their planes hurtled downward in a death dive. And to a Japanese audience, the falling cherry blossoms that mark Keiko's departure from her shrine indicate that she will not live long, but that she will probably die heroically.

[1]Sometimes translated as "the Ah-ness of things," meaning that you barely have time to gasp out an "Ah!" of appreciation before it is gone.

Religious connotations can be even more difficult. Even Americans who know that most Japanese practice a syncretic mixture of Shinto and Buddhism, don't necessarily understand that the two religions have very different emotional connotations. Most Japanese are uninterested in theology. Their religious practices are a matter of tradition, not reasoned analyses or beliefs. And for them, Shinto is a religion of life. They are born Shinto, they marry Shinto, and their loudest, most exuberant festivals are Shinto. The fact that **Vampire Princess Miyu** is first seen sitting on a Shinto gateway (a *torii*) is a tip-off that she is not entirely a creature of death.

In fact, Shinto cannot deal with death which it associates with corruption and decay. When Japanese die, they die Buddhist. For most Japanese, Buddhism is associated with death and funerals. Even cheerful Buddhist festivals such as the *O-Bon* festival which celebrates the return of ancestral spirits during the summer months is associated with death.[2] Kato, the demon of **Doomed Megalopolis**, arrives in Tokyo floating above a river of drifting lanterns launched to honor the dead during the *O-Bon* season. In **The Crystal Triangle**, Buddhist monks are revealed to be hideous, invading aliens. The Japanese are not anti-Buddhist, but the appearance of Buddhist temples, priests or paraphernalia does indicate a somber mood as a rule. Of course, even Americans who know that, still have to be able to tell the difference between a Shinto shrine, usually identified by the *torii* gateway at the front, and a Buddhist temple, usually identified by its Chinese style of architecture featuring pagoda towers and upturned eaves.

[2]This is not true of all Buddhism, just Buddhism as it is practiced in Japan. And even there, Zen Buddhism is an exception. In *anime,* Zen is associated with martial discipline and occasionally with the occult.

Americans may have an even harder time when their own religious traditions are involved. To most Americans, the crucifix is a symbol of goodness and light. Not so in non-Christian Japan. The Japanese are not anti-Christian as a rule, but they regard the religion much as Westerners often regard little understood Asian beliefs, as something exotic, inscrutable, superstitious, and probably linked to the occult. Thus, in **Judge**, when the supernatural attorney for the defense meets with his client in a church and crosses himself on suitable occasions, he is not, as Americans might assume, identifying himself as a good guy. In fact, he is a bit on the sleazy side. His Christian trappings are an indication of his connection with the dark and unknowable. The same is true of Subaru Sumeragi, the androgynous psychic in **Tokyo Babylon** who sometimes wears a cassock reminiscent of a Catholic priest's complete with a large crucifix hanging around his neck. The reference is not to Catholicism or celibacy, but simply to the fact that he possesses supernatural powers. This sort of thing can be confusing and upsetting to American Christians who take their religion seriously.

The significance of holidays also poses problems. Ironically, the worst problems involve those holidays that seem the most familiar. Faced with a Shinto or Buddhist festival, most Americans at least know that they don't know anything about it. They become video tourists, extrapolating information about the event from what they see and hear. That's not the case when *anime* deal with holidays like Valentine's Day or Christmas. They look the same, but they're not. Valentine's Day, for example, comes to Japan complete with doily hearts and chubby cupids. In Japan, however, Valentine's Day is like the American Sadie Hawkins Day. It's the day when women declare their feelings for men. They do this by sending the man of their dreams chocolates. The next move is up to him. That little custom is memorialized at some point or another in almost all *anime* romantic comedies.

Christmas, too, has a different meaning in non-Christian Japan. Santa-san is a popular figure in December and Christmas carols fill the streets. But Christmas in Japan is not focused on the family as it is in the West. (New Year's is the big family festival for the Japanese.) Instead, Christmas is a time for romance. Hotels and restaurants feature elegant Christmas dinners and young men nervously invite young women to be their Christmas date. Many Japanese men pop the question on Christmas Eve. Even if they don't, suggesting or accepting a Christmas date is a sign of serious intent. The exchange of Christmas presents is fraught with romantic tension as, for example, in the "Tendo Family Christmas Scramble" episode of **Ranma 1/2**.

Even cues that are culturally analogous can be confusing if viewers don't recognize what they are being shown. Most Americans, for example, will know that an old Victorian house on a cliff suggests the beginning of a ghost story. They may not realize that the same is true of an old-fashioned, enclosed mansion in the middle of Kyoto, such as that visited by Himiko in the opening sequence of **Vampire Princess Miyu**. They may not realize the house is old-fashioned unless they are familiar with Japanese architecture. Similarly, Americans who could easily deduce from the arrival of a priest bearing bell, book, and candle, that an exorcism or some other supernatural event is in the offing, will ignore such "obvious" hints as in **The Crystal Triangle** when Miyabe suddenly appears wearing a white kimono top with a red divided skirt. Unfortunately, few Americans know that such a costume is the regalia of a *miko*, a Shinto priestess often associated with exorcism and other contacts with the spirit world.

The same is often true of sound cues. *Anime* sound effects frequently make use of Noh or Kabuki traditions such as wooden clappers, drums, and stylized shouts to highlight dramatic moments and build suspense. ***Tenchi Muyō!*** makes very effective use of Kabuki and Noh sound cues whenever the demon Ryōko makes one of her unexpected appearances. The use of wooden clappers in the final sequence of the "Banquet of Marionettes" episode of ***Vampire Princess Miyu*** even more actively recalls theatrical traditions as a doll demon makes off with her human prey. The multicolored curtain that falls behind them is that traditionally used by the Bunraku puppet theater, and thus provides a final grim reference to the fact that both characters have been turned into grotesque puppets. These chilling sound effects work as effectively with Americans as they do with Japanese, but the Americans may well wonder how the Japanese ever thought of doing such a thing. In fact, it took them centuries to come up with just the right sound guaranteed to send shivers up your spine.

With certain other features of *anime*, the cultural barriers are more difficult to overcome and the desired response more difficult to elicit. In erotic moments where American film makers would use a full, swelling orchestra, *anime* may prefer the music of a single *samisen*, a guitar-like instrument associated with the geisha world. In ***Ninja Scroll***, for example, *samisen* music hints at the erotic tension between Jūbei and Kagerō long before the two even touch. Most Americans miss the significance of that sound cue altogether, and even those who understand it rationally may still find the association less than sexually arousing. A movie critic once described *samisen* music as "the sound of a plucked nerve." Because response to sound is so culturally determined, dubbed versions of *anime* sometimes substitute more familiar types of background music and sound effects along with the English voices. Purists disapprove.

In content and style, *anime* also draws heavily on Japanese literary traditions. This is particularly telling in *anime* television series. Unlike American TV which is episodic and fairly static in terms of character development, *anime* created for Japanese television are serial and draw as much of their appeal from character development as from plot. Both approaches have their advantages. The American shows are more versatile in the long run. Each episode is complete in itself and can be rerun in any order. Japanese shows must be run more or less in order. Not only is the plot dependent on a sequential order, but the characters change so dramatically, that mixing and matching is out of the question.

This concern with character analysis over plot should come as no surprise to anyone familiar with Japanese literature. Lady Murasaki set the pace in the late tenth century when she wrote Japan's first novel,

Tale of Genji. On the surface, *Tale of Genji* is an account of the many romances of a charming and promiscuous nobleman and their karmic aftermath. What gives the work its power, however, is its emphasis on personality above plot. Genji is no lust-driven Don Juan; he is a confused and lonely young man whose promiscuity derives largely from his search for the mother he lost in infancy. His downfall is triggered when he begins a semi-incestuous affair with his step-mother, Lady Fujitsubo, who bears an uncanny resemblance to his own dead mother. Genji does eventually grow up, although not in time. Why he does what he does is at least as interesting as what he does, and his personality changes over time. So do the personalities of the women whose lives he affects.

The *anime* version of **Tale of Genji** is visually beautiful and reasonably faithful to the novel. There are a few changes to accommodate modern tastes. Genji is gentler toward young Murasaki and more aggressive toward his wife. The Freudian implications of his obsession with his mother are also highlighted in a series of interludes in which he hides cherry blossoms deep within a dark tree. Unfortunately, most Americans find the *anime* version of **Tale of Genji** difficult to understand. That's partly because the subtitles are difficult to read, but mostly because the movie has a dreamy, drifting quality and scenes follow one another without much explanation or connection. Americans are not sufficiently familiar with the novel to fill in the gaps between scenes. Japanese audiences don't have that problem; *Tale of Genji* is required reading in their schools.

The same problem is apparent even in less literary *anime*. They are based on much longer works, usually *manga,* most of which are not available in English since *manga* translation lags far behind *anime*. Yet, many *anime* assume that their audiences have already read the book. As a result, they may leave out critical background information, particularly background regarding the characters' personalities. That's serious, because character development is as much a part of *anime*'s appeal as plot and action.

Japan's literary tradition has always been heavily introspective. In the action-packed warrior epics of the samurai, the Kabuki romances of the middle class, and even the popular ballads carried from village to village by traveling troubadours, motivation is an important consideration. The same is true in *anime*, and the serial nature of television dramas and OVAs allow it ample time to expand on character development. This also gives *anime* its distinctive moral ambiguity. Since human beings change over time, it's only natural that some villains will reform and become heroes, while some heroes will turn out to have feet of clay.

Character development is the main reason for the success of such *anime* series as **Bubblegum Crisis** and its sequel, **Bubblegum Crash,** an otherwise fairly run-of-the-mill science fiction series about rampaging robots and the power-suited women who fight them. The private lives of the characters of the robot-busting Knight Sabers are what give the series its appeal. Fans enjoy speculating about whether Nene will ever find a boyfriend, whether Priss and Linna are gay, bisexual, or just strongly into female bonding, and whether the cool, intellectual Silia Stingray is even human. This may also tie into the reason why the graphic violence that pervades *anime* does not have the same effect as violence on American television. If the emphasis is on personality, violence cannot be without results. That was apparent in one episode of **Bubblegum Crisis** when Priss was compelled to kill Sylvie, a young woman she loved. Sylvie was an android and programmed to kill. At the end, she begged Priss to kill her before she did any more damage. Although Priss did what was necessary, the incident left her a psychological basket case, and there was a real question about whether she would be able to continue her crime-fighting activities. Although Priss eventually rejoined the Knight Sabers, she was a changed woman. And she has never changed back or forgotten. The message is clear. No one kills with impunity, not even when she's the hero and her act is completely justified.

The same emphasis on personality explains the popularity of **Battle Angel**, a bleak saga of an amnesiac cyborg's search for love in a dystopic universe. The protagonist, Gally (renamed Alita in the translated *manga*), may have lost her memory, but her programmed defense instincts are lethal enough to assure her personal survival. That doesn't mean there is no suspense, however. Gally's own strength means that she struggles on while those she loves fall by the wayside. The mood grows bleaker and bleaker as Gally's emptied memory refills with the faces of those she has loved and lost. How long can she continue to cope with so many losses? Tune in next episode and find out.

Character development need not be traumatic, of course. The humor of **Ranma** $^1/_2$ derives as much from the personalities of the characters as it does from bizarre plot twists and slapstick martial arts. It's not just that the characters are so unusual in themselves. The improbable pairing of tomboyish, boy-hating Akane with an inarticulate roughneck like Ranma would have comic possibilities even if he didn't change sex whenever he was splashed with cold water. However, those possibilities would soon be exhausted if the characters remained static. The reason **Ranma *¹/₂*** has run for so many years is the development not only of the characters, but also of their relationships to one another. And that doesn't just apply to the main characters. Of course, it's entertaining to wonder whether Akane and Ranma will ever admit their love to each other or even to themselves. But there are other characters to watch too. There's Ryōga whose unrequited love for Akane slowly changes to friendship. There's Kasumi, the stereotypical Japanese woman, whose gentle virtues attract few followers other than the daffy Dr. Tofu. Will she ever find fulfillment? There's Shampoo, the Chinese amazon, whose aggressive pursuit of Ranma is doomed to failure. Will she never acknowledge the devotion of Mousse, the martial artist with the Coke-bottle glasses? The possibilities are endless and so is the series.

All this has a price. Being an *otaku* takes work. Not only do you have to adjust to an alien dramatic form, you also have to keep an eye on what's happening. You can't just tune in and out whenever you feel like it.

Why do young Americans stick with an art form that is so foreign and so difficult to understand, an art form that actually makes them work? Generation X's image does not usually include much emphasis on the work ethic. Yet, this is the generation that has chosen to tackle a challenging art form purely for the purpose of entertainment. One reason, of course, is that the Baby Busters simply aren't as lazy as Boomer curmudgeons would like to believe. The other reason, however, is that *anime* more than repays the effort by providing its fans with a fantasy world more compelling and more complete than they can find anywhere else. Okay, it's escapism, but for a generation whose defining characteristic is that they are the first set of Americans who will not do as well as their parents, good escapism is worth a little effort.

And *anime* is escapism raised to a high art. Created for a society where personal behavior is severely constrained both by physical crowding and strict social conventions, *anime* is designed to provide a wide range of fantasy worlds where audiences can live out dreams (and sometimes nightmares) that will never otherwise find expression. Whether it's an alien planet inhabited by robots, a rural paradise complete with elves, a supernatural world inhabited by gods and demons, or an ordinary Japanese neighborhood coping with unruly adolescents and alien invaders, Japanese animators have a real talent for creating believable environments and creatures for their fantasies.

In this stress-filled, postmodern world people need fantasies, especially adults. Yet Americans are loath to admit that. They visit Disneyland and other theme parks in record numbers, but always insisting that these fantasies are "for the kids." Most people bring kids along just to prove that point. Perhaps this reluctance on the part of American adults to unabashedly participate in play and fantasy is due to the Puritan heritage and its injunction to adults to "put away childish things." Perhaps it's simply the quest of a young nation to seem more mature than it is. Either way, this national reluctance ignores the fundamental fact that all human beings, regardless of age, need to play. Fortunately, the Japanese, who are neither Puritans nor from a particularly young nation, have provided a wonderful toy in *anime*.

Chapter Three

Other Gods, Other Demons

Where do anime creators get their ideas? Why did Masaki Kajishima, creator of **Tenchi Muyō!**, suddenly decide that trees with ropes tied around their tummies could fly space ships, or that a cute little cabbit (half cat, half rabbit) might actually be a space ship? What possessed Narumi Kakinouchi, author of **Vampire Princess Miyu,** to dream up the *shinma,* those tragic creatures who are simultaneously gods and demons, and whose stories are often as heartbreaking as they are horrible. What subconscious depths led Yūzō Takada to create Pai, the half girl, half monster heroine of **3 X 3 Eyes** ? Why, when Rumiko Takahashi needed to create a kidnap scene for **Trouble in Nekonron China**, the first Ranma movie, did she come up with a flying Chinese treasure ship loaded with seven lucky (and bizarre) gods? Why would Kōsuke Fujishima want to bedevil Tokyo with Norse goddesses? And why would anyone portray Jehovah as a green caterpillar?

33

These are just a few of the questions that sometimes lead American *otaku* to conclude that Japanese animators are severely disturbed if not actually mentally ill. In fact, Japanese animators are no nuttier than any other group of creative people. What they are doing is little different from what American writers of science fiction and fantasy do every day. They are retelling their ancient myths and legends in modern form, retailoring their old religious and heroic traditions to conform to modern ideas about who and what they are. The reason their creations seem so bizarre to Americans is because they are drawing their material from an entirely different cultural tradition. Most of the old myths being used are completely unfamiliar to Americans. The stories may be old, but Americans haven't heard them yet.

The largest number of stories are drawn from Shinto, Japan's indigenous religion. Shinto is an animistic form of nature worship which provides *anime* with over eight million deities and their legends from which to draw on. Shinto itself is quite alien to the Judeo-Christian concept of organized religion. Indeed, Shinto could best be described as disorganized religion. It has no official theology, no set scriptures, and no moral code beyond cleanliness. What Shinto does have, however, is stories, over 2,000 years worth of stories about gods and goddesses, heroes and scoundrels, noble souls and tricksters.

Often those categories overlap since a Shinto deity, called a *kami*, is nothing like the Western idea of a god. This can lead to some serious misconceptions even with subtitled *anime*, where *kami* or *kamisama* (honorable *kami*) is often translated as "God." In fact, the deity or deities being appealed to are far more nebulous, far less anthropomorphic, and certainly less Judeo-Christian than the translation suggests.

A *kami* is the essence or soul of anything that inspires awe. An impressive mountain or a beautiful waterfall can be a *kami*. An ancient tree, an oddly shaped rock, and almost all animals can be *kami*. Watch out for foxes, raccoons, rabbits, and cats in particular; they are tricksters of Shinto. Human emotions such as anger, jealousy, or mirth can be *kami*. So can abstract qualities like war, fertility, and mercy. And of course, people can be *kami*. The Emperor is obviously a very powerful *kami*, but lesser mortals such as General Nogi who won the Russo-Japanese War in 1905 and committed *seppuku*[1] to follow his Emperor in death are also *kami* and have shrines dedicated to them. And there are the older *kami* drawn from

[1]Westerners often refer to these ritual suicides as *harakiri*. In fact, *harakiri* literally means "belly slitting," an accurate description of what is actually done, but distinctly lacking in respect. The term *harakiri* is most often used by critics of the practice.

Japan's prehistory whose stories still have the power to move modern Japanese. Shinto alone provides Japanese animators with hundreds of stories.

Shinto stories form such a basic part of any Japanese childhood that *anime* artists evoke them often without conscious thought, and they are accepted in the same spirit by Japanese audiences. But what about American audiences? They may not recognize Japan's ancient *kami* or the new forms they take in anime, but they do recognize the emotional power of these old stories.

That comes as a shock to many Japanese who like to think of Shinto as "unique." In fact, it is not. Shinto's animistic gods and their legends are similar to those found in most early cultures. What is unique to Shinto is the fact that it has survived relatively unchanged into the modern era. The Europeans burned their pagan heritage at the stake during the middle ages. Other cultures lost their traditions or saw them twisted to suit Western imperialist rhetoric in the eighteenth and nineteenth centuries. Some of this happened to Shinto too when the legend of the Sun Goddess was used to build a new nationalism. For the most part, however, the Japanese have preserved intact their ability to dance half naked on a hillside in celebration of the wondrous and incomprehensible. Moreover, they are able to get up the next day, go in to the office and cope with the needs of the late twentieth century without any sense of discontinuity. They are either the last true pagans or the first completely successful postmodernists!

The Shinto ability to blend the fantastic with the everyday is basic to Japanese life and to the world of *anime*. And it is one of the features that makes *anime* so attractive to young Americans, especially those who are interested in alternate forms of spirituality. Many *otaku* are also interested in New Age neo-paganism and neo-mysticism. Shinto, of course, is not neo-anything. It's the real thing.

Nor is it foolish or superficial for Americans to learn about Shinto through a medium like *anime*. Shinto has always been communicated through stories presented as much for their entertainment value as to transmit historical or cultural values. Indeed, since Shinto lacks any set texts or gospel, most Japanese do not differentiate between the early myths recounted in ancient texts like the *Nihongi* or *Kojiki* and related "fairy tales" like "Urashima Tarō," "The Snow Maiden," or "The Princess of the Bamboo Grove."[2] This troubles Americans who have been

[2]Urashima Tarō is a Rip Van Winkle–like character. The Snow Maiden is a beautiful woman who seduces and then freezes her lovers to death. Lady Kaguya, the Princess of the Bamboo Grove, was born from the heart of a bamboo, broke the heart of an Emperor, and was finally carried off to rule on the moon.

raised in a Judeo-Christian tradition that insists on a strict differentiation between sacred and secular writings. It shouldn't. It doesn't bother the Japanese and these are, after all, their stories.

Shinto has something else to offer young Americans. Religion may be on the rise among Generation X, but so is the demand for greater tolerance. Most young Americans choose a religion because it fills their personal spiritual needs. They are distressed when they find that their choice has alienated family and friends who have made a different choice. The syncretism they sense in *anime* is alien to Western culture, but appealing to someone growing up in the multicultural world of late twentieth-century America.

One reason Shinto has survived as well as it has is its ability to exist in harmony with other doctrines. Early in Japan's history, Buddhist missionaries brought their faith to the land of the rising sun. Instead of Buddhism's arrival causing the religious wars Westerners would expect in such a situation, Shinto and Buddhism merged. Monks worked out elaborate charts in which Buddhist saints were presented as the heavenly incarnations of more earthly Shinto deities. Later, Buddhist temples and Shinto shrines sometimes occupied the same space. The monastery of Kiyomizu in Kyoto, for example, was built around the older shrine to Okuninushi, the Shinto god of virility, and his rabbit companion, the White Hare of Inaba. Today, the Buddhist monks go serenely about their celibate business, undisturbed by the presence of this lustful pair in their midst. Shinto charms are often offered for sale at Buddhist festivals and vice versa. The result is the syncretic mix practiced by most Japanese today. Such syncretism goes far beyond mere tolerance. It represents real acceptance.

And that acceptance did not end with Buddhism. Over the years, the Japanese have added Taoism, Confucianism, elements of Hinduism and, most recently, Christianity to their spiritual storehouse. Christian missionaries are often dismayed to find that their new converts see no problem in hanging a crucifix on the wall beside the family shrine, just above the statue of the Buddha. That mix-and-match attitude is most evident in Japan's new religions. Adherents of the Ryūgu Otohime shrine near Kyoto, for example, revere their founder as the incarnation of the Shinto sea goddess, the Princess of the Dragon Palace. They also equate Jehovah with the Japanese wind god Susanō, worship both Christ and the Torah, and insist that there can be no harmony on Earth until matriarchy is restored and the Jews are at peace in Israel. That's a mix even Southern California can't top.

That real life eclecticism finds even greater expression in *anime.* Unfettered by any claims to serious theology, *anime* artists feel no compunctions about adding archaic beliefs such as Greco-Roman, Mayan, or Teutonic mythology to this mythological stew. In **Silent Möbius,** for example, Katsumi Liqueur draws pentagrams in her own blood and calls upon the Sun Goddess, the archangels, and several Greek deities in her efforts to exorcize Lucifer Hawk. In *Judge,* a supernatural courtroom is set upon a huge mandala with the ten Buddhist kings of Hell in attendance, but the attorney for the defense operates out of a Christian church and crosses himself in moments of stress. In the comedy **Oh, My Goddess!**, a Norse goddess accidentally summoned to modern Tokyo calls on the spirits of a ruined Buddhist temple to provide a home for herself and the Japanese college student she loves. Another comedy, **Urusei Yatsura,** features an incompetent Shinto priestess, her equally inept uncle who is a Buddhist monk, her boyfriend who has studied Satanism in the West, and a variety of non-humans with super powers who are variously identified as extraterrestrials, gods, or demons. And just in case that isn't enough, *anime* artists sometimes make up new deities. For example, Pai, the three-eyed immortal with the split personality in **3 X 3 Eyes,** is a complete invention although her powers and her third eye owe something to Buddhist, Hindu, and Tibetan beliefs.

The revival of interest in ancient mythologies is not unique to Japan. In America, too, fantasy novels based on ancient Celtic, Greek, or other Western mythologies are popular with young adults. And Western authors have also begun to experiment with combining different mythologies to produce something new. Tom Robbin's *Jitterbug Perfume,* for example, combined Greek and Teutonic mythologies with Voodoo and Tantric Buddhism. Neil Gaiman populated his graphic novel, *The Sandman,* with characters drawn from all the Western traditions, including Christianity. Even the Japanese sent Susanō, the Shinto wind god, as a representative to *The Sandman's* gathering of deities.

American television has also begun to experiment with retelling ancient Western myths for modern audiences. Inspired by the success of sword and sorcery movie fantasies, network TV has recently brought such shows as **Hercules** and **Xena: Warrior Princess** to the screen. Both shows combine elements of mythology with new plots and characters, seasoning the whole mix with anachronistic, often trendy humor. That's very much in the *anime* tradition, although more rigid

American strictures regarding violence, sex, and death prevent them from developing their material to the fullest. The fact that these shows also use live actors also limits the extent to which the fantastic can be made to seem natural. Whether or not Americans will accept these new arrivals on the American TV scene remains to be seen.

These American efforts are actually more suited to their audiences than *anime* will ever be. They use traditions that are far more familiar to American audiences. The trouble is, this kind of eclectic fantasy is very new in America, and so far the output is small. *Anime* provides an immediate and prolific alternative. Unfortunately, most Americans are completely unfamiliar with the mythologies used by Japanese animators. That has its advantages. *Anime* often seems more creative to Americans than it does to Japanese simply because their source material is so unfamiliar.

But Americans also miss out because of their unfamiliarity with Asian myths. An appreciation of the way in which a really good animator has redefined and combined mythologies is one of the pleasures of watching *anime*. American *otaku* can probably never hope to equal the instinctive recognition with which Japanese identify the mythological elements in *anime*, but a basic understanding of some of the myths that appear most frequently is an easier project.

The ancient Shinto myths developed as an oral tradition. In the eighth century, when the Japanese first began to write using Chinese characters, the first thing they did was to transcribe their ancient myths. These still exist in two versions, the *Nihongi* and the *Kojiki,* and they are available in translation. They make difficult reading, however. This is partly because of their antiquity, but mostly because the translations currently in print date from the turn of the century and the authors opted to switch to Latin whenever they hit one of the naughty bits. Since early Shinto legends have a lot of naughty bits, the result is very disjointed for anyone who is not fully literate in Latin. More readable versions of the myths also exist in English, but most of these have been retold as fairy stories and edited to make them suitable for children. A readable, unembarrassed translation of the *Nihongi* and the *Kojiki* is badly needed, especially by American *otaku.*

Anime pulls heavily on those old legends. For example, the story of the Sun Goddess, Amaterasu, and her brother, Susanō, forms the basis for **Tenchi Muyō!**, but in such an indirect fashion that no one who is not fully familiar with the original would recognize it. There is no danger of that with a Japanese audience. This story is as familiar to them as the story of Adam and Eve is to Americans regardless of whether they are Christians or have ever even read the Bible. That, in fact, is what makes **Tenchi Muyō!** so effective. The power of the old legend combined with the skill and humor of contemporary *anime* produces a new form difficult to define as either serious drama or comedy, science fiction or fantasy.

The original story of Amaterasu and Susanō is recorded in both the *Nihongi* and the *Kojiki*.[3] They were brother and sister, born of Izanami and Izanagi, the two original gods who created both the islands of Japan and its myriad deities. Izanami and Izanagi were brother and sister, but they were also married. Amaterasu and Susanō never went through any formal marriage ceremony. Indeed, Susanō later married someone else. However, he and his sister did produce a number of children together, including the line that eventually became Japan's Imperial family. Sadly, moments of love were rare for them. Mostly, they fought.

Their most famous fight occurred when Susanō visited his sister on the high plains of Heaven. Ostensibly, his purpose was to apologize for an earlier incident, but she suspected him from the start. Her suspicions were confirmed by his behavior. He trampled her rice paddies and defiled her palace by defecating beneath her throne. The last straw, however, was when he flung a flayed colt into her weaving room, causing her to wound herself with her own shuttle.[4] Deeply offended, Amaterasu retired to the rock cave of Heaven, pulled a huge rock across the entrance and stayed there, leaving the Earth without sunlight. The planet began to die.

The other gods realized something had to be done. They decided to play on Amaterasu's curiosity and her love of a good time by holding a huge party outside her cave. They guessed that she would be unable to resist peeking out to see what was going on and they were right. The party reached its climax when Uzume, the Dread Female of Heaven, got up on top of an upturned sake barrel and began to strip. Her dance caused such an uproar, especially from the male deities present, that Amaterasu just had to find out what was happening. As she peeked out, the Force god seized her and dragged her the rest of the way. The other gods sealed up the entrance so that she could not return. Amaterasu was at first annoyed, but when she realized the damage her sulking had caused,

[3]Actually there are many versions of this story in both books. Since the eighth-century scribes were listening to oral traditions from all over Japan and had no way of determining which was closest to the original, they wrote them all down.

[4]Scholars differ on why this was such an unforgivable offense, although most agree that the combination of death and blood represents serious pollution, a major consideration in Shinto where cleanliness is not just next to godliness; it is godliness.

she forgave them. Susanō was expelled from Heaven. He went to Earth where he had many adventures and even became something of a hero. Later he became the lord of the underworld.[5] Eventually, even his sister forgave him.

In the 1950s, Osamu Tezuka produced a *manga* version of Shinto mythology in the first volume of *Hi no Tori* ("phoenix" or "firebird"), a long running saga of reincarnation and the search for immortality that began in the remote past and continued into the far future. In the first volume, however, Tezuka stuck to the old myths, which he combined with archeological and historical data to try to produce a story of what might really have happened. In *Hi no Tori*, Amaterasu is recast as a semi-historical figure, Queen Himiko.

Himiko reigned in the first century A.D., long before the Japanese began to record their own history. Her reign was documented by a Chinese sea captain who described her as an older woman who lived apart from her people attended by a thousand women and one man. She was a shaman, a priestess who went into trances during which time the gods spoke with her voice. When she died, a man tried to take her throne. The people would not accept him, however, and revolted. Finally Himiko's niece, a thirteen-year-old girl named Iyo, took the throne and order was restored. Himiko's story, along with other accounts of female shaman queens and empresses has sparked a debate among Japanese scholars as to whether early Japan was a matriarchy.

Hi no Tori presents a middle view. In Tezuka's version, prehistoric Japan is composed of many different tribes. Some, like Himiko's, are matriarchies while others are ruled by men. Tezuka's depiction of Himiko's rule is unlikely to please feminists. His Himiko/Amaterasu is a charlatan who controls her people by preying on their superstitions. Her brother, still named Susanō, acts as her advisor. From the first he is resentful of her power, critical of her judgment, and frustrated by her refusal to let him marry. Tezuka only hinted at the possibility that brother and sister were sexually involved.[6] Nonetheless, it is jealousy over his sister's flirtation with a handsome archer that precipitates Susanō's final outburst. Heartbroken and furious, he tries to drown his sorrows in drink. He is, in fact, dead drunk when he hurls a dead cow into his sister's chambers. Queen

[5]Early Christian missionaries tried to equate Susanō with Satan or at least, with Lucifer. This is inaccurate. Susanō is not evil. He is a wind god. He blows, sometimes destructively. His sister is not entirely free from faults either. Like all Shinto gods, Amaterasu and Susanō are too human to ever represent pure evil or, for that matter, pure good.

[6]The original myth, other Shinto myths, and some archeological, ethnographic, and historical analyses of this period suggest some form of brother-sister marriage. This, like the question of whether or not early Japan was a matriarchy, is a hotly contested issue which incites strong emotions as well as opinions on all sides.

Himiko's response is not as moderate as that of the original Amaterasu. Instead of retiring, she has his eyes burned out with molten lead. Soon thereafter, a solar eclipse occurs. Interpreting this as divine retribution for her attack on her brother, Himiko flees to a cave where she cowers in terror. When the eclipse ends, she emerges and manages to claim credit for the return of the sun. The *manga* version of *Hi no Tori* has never been published in English translation, probably because a full appreciation of it requires a better knowledge of Shinto myths and early Japanese history than most Americans possess.

A subtitled, live-action version of *Hi no Tori* is available under the title **The Phoenix** from Video Action in Los Angeles. This movie version of *Hi no Tori* was one of Tezuka's experimental films. It combines live action with animation including some unrelated and inappropriate cameo appearances by Astro Boy. The experiment was not a total success. The movie is overly long, and the enjoyment for English speakers is further impaired by the fact that the subtitles are difficult to read.

The story of how Amaterasu was lured out of her cave by the gods also appears in a much less serious form in an early episode of **Maison Ikkoku,** a bittersweet love story by Rumiko Takahashi that plays in a run-down Tokyo boarding house. In the Takahashi version, a young student named Yūsaku is trying desperately to study for his university entrance exams. His fellow boarders are determined to have him join in a party to celebrate the arrival of a beautiful new landlady. Yūsaku avoids them by locking himself in a closet with his books. They lure him out by pretending that Ryōko, the landlady, is performing a striptease. Yūsaku, who is already hopelessly in love with her, can't resist peeking. As soon as he does so, the others pull him out. His study time is over. Worse, it takes several more episodes to convince Ryōko that he is not an indiscriminate letch.

Of course, it is quite possible to enjoy this episode of **Maison Ikkoku** without noticing the Shinto reference. The story works regardless. However, the skill with which Takahashi blends Shinto and other myths into her work is part of what makes her so popular. Indeed, Shinto references pervade her **Urusei Yatsura** series which is probably what makes it so difficult for American audiences, despite AnimEigo's excellent liner notes.

Yet most of the Shinto references in **Urusei Yatsura** are fairly direct and can be looked up by anyone with a good book about Japanese mythology and the ability to use an index. If they buy the tape or rent one that still includes the liner notes, they won't even have to do that. Either way, they will soon discover where characters such as Baku, the dream-eating demon in **Beautiful Dreamer,** the *kappa* who pull Ataru into their pool, and the *tengu* who serve Kurama, the crow princess, come from. They will also learn about the vampire-like reputation of the Snow Maiden who Takahashi recasts as Oyuki, the queen of Neptune, whose need for snow shovelers leads to some major interdimensional kidnaping. They will learn that Inaba, the apprentice time bunny who gets Ataru, Lum, and Shinobu lost between alternate futures in the first **Urusei Yatsura** OVA, is named for the White Hare of Inaba, one of Shinto's more notorious tricksters and a fertility symbol to boot! And, of course, they will learn that when Ataru refers to Lum and her family as *oni,* he is not simply noting their extraterrestrial origins. He is using a word that also refers to Japanese demons.

Masaki Kajishima goes further in **Tenchi Muyō!** The references to Shinto legend are unmistakable, but the story and characters have been changed. Moreover, later episodes incorporated a large number of non-Shinto elements. In the first few episodes, however, the references were clear. While spending his summer vacation at his grandfather's Shinto shrine, a young man named Tenchi releases a demon that was imprisoned by his own ancestor, Yosho,[7] centuries before. Indeed, the family traditionally serves at that shrine in order to keep the demon locked safely away. The demon turns out to be a rather attractive green-haired woman named Ryōko who falls in love with Tenchi. Unfortunately, Ryōko is a self-proclaimed sadist and her brand of love seems likely to be lethal. Worse yet, her release has triggered the sacred tree of Tenchi's family shrine to send out a warning beacon. That beacon is heard by Ayeka, a princess of the planet Jurai, who has been searching the galaxy for her brother, Yosho. Yosho was to have married her, but when the demon (alternatively described as a space pirate) Ryōko attacked Jurai, he ran off in pursuit and was never seen again. The beacon which signals the presence of Ryōko is her first lead in years, and soon she too is on Tenchi's doorstep demanding to see a man who has been dead for centuries. She too falls in love with Tenchi and, although she affects very ladylike manners, her stuffy arrogance and bad temper also bode ill for the young man's peace of mind.

[7]Kajishima, the creator of **Tenchi Muyō!** insists that the names are drawn from various place names in his native Okayama prefecture and that Yosho comes from Mount Yosho. Perhaps, but the name may also be a reference to a ninth-century Buddhist mountain recluse reputed to have become an immortal being with supernatural powers. **Tenchi Muyō!**'s Yosho does have these attributes, but does not share the original Yosho's taste for piety and asceticism.

Tenchi Muyō! is filled with Shinto references. Ayeka's ship and that of her younger sister, Sasami, are controlled by huge space trees which are, in fact, sacred trees complete down to the plaited ropes (*shimenawa*) and hung with white paper chains (*nigite* or *nusa*). The same is true of the shrine's tree which sends out the warning beacon. Later, it is revealed to be the tree that piloted Yosho's ship. However, it has taken root and can no longer fly.

The plaited ropes that identify the space trees in **Tenchi Muyō!** are closely connected to the legend of Amaterasu and Susanō. The first *shimenawa* was strung across the opening to the rock cave of Heaven in order to prevent the Sun Goddess from returning. Today, the *shimenawa* are used to purify and sanctify objects and places. To gird a tree with such a rope is to acknowledge that it is a *kami*. Trees girded with *shimenawa* are a regular sight in the Japanese countryside.[8] *Shimenawa* are also used to mark off sacred places and as wards to keep evil out . . . or in.

Tenchi Muyō! is also filled with images of swords, jewels, and mirrors. Tenchi's troubles begin when he removes an old sword from a shrine hung with *shimenawa*. The sword, which controls him more than the other way around, is not only a weapon, but a key to an unknown variety of supernatural powers and a symbol of Tenchi's extraterrestrial connections. It also allows him some control over Ryoko because it can bestow or remove the jewels from which she draws her powers. Ryōko's spaceship, Ryō-Ohki, is also dependent on jewels. Most of the time Ryō-Ohki takes the form of a cabbit, a cute, furry animal that seems to be a cross between a cat and a rabbit. When danger threatens, however, she[9] becomes a ship powered by floating circles of red-pink gems. Those gems are each capable of manifesting as individual cabbits as Tenchi discovers when they invade his carrot supply. Mirrors do not appear as such, but there is a strong emphasis on mirror worlds. Washu is held captive in one such mirror world aboard Kagato's ship, and Sasami contacts another mirror world when she needs to summon her ship, *Tsunami,* which is also an older, mirror version of herself.

This obsession with sword, jewel, and mirror is no accident. These are the three sacred treasures of Japan and powerful reminders of Shinto mythology and Japan's prehistory.

[8] For a clearer idea of how such sacred trees are ordinarily regarded and included in religious life by the Japanese, take a look at the "King of the Forest" tree in **My Neighbor Totoro.**

[9] Gender is difficult to determine in the case of creatures like Ryō-Ohki. However, when she later takes semi-human form, she is female and since she was created from the same genetic experiment that created Ryoko, it's hard to see how she could be anything else. Ryō-Ohki takes a male form in the **Pretty Sammy** spin-off, but that's an alternate story line. In any case, even inanimate, ocean-going ships get called "she."

The original sacred sword is said to be the one used by Susanō to defeat the eight-headed dragon. The jewels are a necklace said to belong to Amaterasu, the Sun Goddess. The mirror is also held to be Amaterasu's and to hold her image. According to some versions of the story, it was also used to lure her from her cave. The usual archeological interpretation is that these three treasures represent prized items acquired by Japan's prehistoric rulers through trade or war with the technologically more advanced cultures of China and Korea. By constantly bombarding his audience with such clearly identifiable images, Kajishima is asking them to recognize both the original myths and his version of them. That undoubtedly works well with Japanese audiences, but Americans unfamiliar with the myths are often just confused.

[10]Kajishima has taken full advantage of this in later spin-offs such as the TV series and the ***Pretty Sammy*** series which cast the same characters in completely different story lines.

What Kajishima has done with Shinto myth in ***Tenchi Muyō!*** is similar to what many American science fiction writers do with Western traditions when they suggest that angels or Greek gods may actually have been visitors from space. Kajishima has, however, taken more liberties than most American writers would find comfortable, possibly because he is more confident of his audience's ability to spot the mythological references. Moreover, the fact that Shinto is still being practiced and therefore constantly being revised gives him additional latitude. So does the fact that between the *Nihongi* and the *Kojiki*, there are at least ten slightly different versions of this particular myth.[10]

[11]The name translates literally as "thick mist sword," and refers to the mists in which it and the dragon lived before Susanō came on the scene. Japanese swords often have personal names indicating that they are considered at least sentient if not actually *kami*. This is not unknown in the West although it is less common. Excalibur is probably the best known sword with a name in European traditions.

In any case, ***Tenchi Muyō!*** is not, strictly speaking, a retelling of the myth anyway. Or if it is, the implication is that the early Japanese seriously misunderstood what the aliens and/or gods were really doing. Ayeka is not really Amaterasu despite her arrival from the stars and her search for a brother who is also a husband. Nor is Yosho, when he finally turns up, really Susanō. He is a rather gentle soul although a twinkle in his eye suggests he could create major chaos if he chose. However, his early legend of having defeated the demon Ryōko and locked her away in the cave does correspond to one of Susanō's later adventures when he rescued a young woman about to be eaten by an eight-headed dragon. He triumphed by getting the dragon drunk on *sake* and then chopping off its heads while it slept. As a reward, he got the girl and also a magical sword named *Murakumo-no-Tsurugi* which he gave to his sister as an apology.[11]

(Takahashi used the legend of Susanō and the dragon to good effect in the "An Akane to Remember" episode of her **Ranma ¹/₂** series. In Takahashi's irreverent version, however, cross-dressing replaced the trick with the *sake* and the sword became a push broom. **Blue Seed** also begins with a straightforward version of this myth before branching off into pure science fiction. There the eight-headed dragon becomes a race of alien shape-shifters, the Aragami.)

Tenchi Muyō!'s Ryōko has only one head, of course, but her demeanor is often worthy of a dragon and she undoubtedly shares the beast's taste for *sake*. She also has some of the characteristics of Uzume, the Dread Female of Heaven, whose striptease lured Amaterasu from her cave. She certainly has that deity's rowdy lack of modesty and also her talent for annoying and manipulating Amatersu/Ayeka. However, she also pulls most of her power from the jewels in her wrists, a factor that might link her to the Sun Goddess. Of course, if Ryōko represents any part of Amaterasu, the whole question of who started what in that original battle with Susanō/Yosho back on planet Jurai needs to be reexamined!

To many Americans, taking such liberties with a religion seems irreverent if not actually sacrilegious. But the truth is, most Japanese are irreverent about their native religion, at least if their behavior is judged by Western standards. Many young Japanese deny any belief in Shinto at all. If asked, they refer to it as a crude collection of outdated superstitions. Yet, most of them attend Shinto festivals, dangle Shinto charms from their backpacks, and sometimes leave a small offering at the local shrine. If pressed, most of them will explain that this is matter of carrying on family traditions, not of personal belief. Most Americans who live in Japan for any length of time learn to be skeptical of such assertions. The usual Japanese attitude toward their native religion is actually a sophisticated mixture of rational cynicism and a deliberate suspension of disbelief. It also involves a recognition of the greater abstractions behind the ancient stories, the fact that a complete rejection of the Shinto gods would also mean rejecting an entire way of life, perhaps an entire world view. Young Japanese, who have long since despaired of trying to explain that to literal-minded Westerners, usually sum it up as simple atheism.

For many Westerners, however, the sight of their first Shinto festival seems to bear out the stated atheism of many of its practitioners. To Western eyes, Shinto festivities look more like a party than a church service. Shinto simply is not a religion of hushed voices and humble supplication. Shinto festivals are loud, often bawdy events usually fueled by *sake*, beer, and whiskey. Even prayer at a Shinto shrine is noisy. Worshippers ring a bell and clap twice before the shrine to ensure that the deity is listening and their efforts are not wasted. (Tenchi does this in the opening episode of **Tenchi Muyō!** after he thinks he has blown Ryōko up in a gas explosion; to his horror, she answers his summons.) Children run freely about the shrine grounds and no one tells them to be quiet. Shinto, after all, is a celebration of life.

But there is a darker side to Shinto. That is apparent even in a relatively cheerful rendition like **Tenchi Muyō!.** Tenchi, a fairly typical young Japanese, is anything but thrilled to find his ancient deities on his doorstep, and downright reluctant to acknowledge his relationship to them.[12] That fear of Japan's ancient gods is more explicitly defined in the prologue to **Vampire Princess Miyu.** As the opening credits roll, a somber male voice explains that:

> At one time, gods and demons were as one. They were sealed away in the abyss of ancient memory. The hearts of humans who feared the Dark brought this about. For the present, let us call these beings *shinma*.[13] Now they have awakened from their slumber and gathered in the Dark. On the final night of that gathering, when *shinma* and humans met again, a young girl strayed into their midst. This is her story. Her name is (pause) Vampire Princess Miyu.

To Americans who like to divide their *dramatis personae* into good guys and bad guys, that seems to suggest that in this series at least, the ancient gods have become demons to be defeated by the heroine, Miyu. It's not that simple. Miyu does indeed do battle with the *shinma,* driving them back into the Dark whenever they emerge to terrorize humanity, but she does so for her own inscrutable reasons which might change at any time. And there is every reason to suspect Miyu's motives. Although she takes the form of a pretty young girl, she is still a vampire with a vampire's thirst. Her bite is not lethal, of course. It's worse. Miyu leaves her victims with an eternal life utterly devoid of meaning. She is herself a *shinma.*

And she's not the only one. Despite the statement in the opening narration, **Vampire Princess Miyu** is not exclusively Miyu's story. It is also the story of Se Himiko, an earnest young medium who hunts both Miyu and the *shinma.* That Himiko is named for Japan's ancient

[12]It should be noted that the Japanese creation myths are very different from their Judeo-Christian counterparts in that the Japanese see themselves, their land, and all other living things as being descended from and still connected to the gods, not as separate artifacts of creation.

[13]*Shinma* is a new word created by combining the character for "god" with the character for "demon." To Japanese, that speaks for itself.

shaman queen is no accident. This is not a common woman's name in contemporary Japan. The name is a tip-off that Himiko, too, is supernatural in some way, possibly yet another *shinma*. In **Vampire Princess Miyu,** as in most *anime*, the issue is never as simple as good versus evil.

The *shinma* also have their stories, many of them quite sympathetic. For example, in the "A Banquet of Marionettes" episode, Miyu's opponent is a female *shinma* who takes the form of a wooden doll and who turns her victims into dolls, thereby trapping their life-force for later consumption. The episode begins at a high school where the *shinma* is masquerading as an unusually lovely schoolgirl. She has already killed one of her female classmates, and is now engaged in seducing a beautiful schoolboy named Kei. Miyu's task is to rescue Kei from the clutches of this monster, seemingly a worthy goal. But the situation is more complex than that. Kei, it turns out, has already recognized the *shinma*'s true nature. He loves her anyway and goes willingly to his fate. Moreover, Miyu's motives are far from altruistic. She also loves Kei and wants him for her own less than commendable pleasures. Far from being a battle between good and evil, this is simply an eternal triangle. Very eternal. And a similar emotional and moral ambivalence toward the supernatural and spiritual pervades this entire, extremely popular series.

Urusei Yatsura, for all its playful zaniness, also lumps gods and demons together indiscriminately. Initially, the two seem to be fairly clearly labeled. Lum and her relatives who begin the series by parking their spaceship above a normal Japanese neighborhood and challenging the local high school lecher to a game of tag, are called *oni,* a term which may refer to their planet of origin in the context of the series, but it definitely refers to demons in any other context.

Oni appear regularly in Japanese folklore. In the original versions, they are fearsome creatures, often gigantic in size, with prolific, oddly colored hair, and horns. They are supernaturally strong, able to fly, and often dress in tiger-skin loincloths. They have enormous appetites which is unfortunate since they eat human beings. They also desire human beings sexually, and often carry them off against their will. Such abductions are usually the work of a male *oni* with a female human victim, but there are some stories of female *oni* who carry off handsome young men.

In **Urusei Yatsura,** Takahashi skillfully combines these ancient *oni* legends with other aspects of Japanese folklore and modern science fiction to produce the total insanity that results when a female *oni* named Lum falls in love with a Japanese high school student named Ataru. Technically speaking, Lum conforms to the traditional description of an *oni*. She has small horns and green hair. She is able to fly and dresses in a tiger-skin bikini. She is neither gigantic nor ugly, but her father is. Her *oni* fiancé, Rei, fills in the final aspect of the traditional *oni* by possessing an enormous appetite, although fortunately his cravings extend more to beef bowls[14] than to human flesh. All the *oni* have some sort of supernatural power. Lum's is the ability to emit a powerful electrical charge which she uses to keep the eternally lecherous Ataru in line, more or less.

However, Lum and her *oni* relations aren't the only ones who arrive to bedevil Ataru and his family. According to the Shinto priestess, Miss Sakura, and her uncle, a Buddhist monk named Cherry,[15] Ataru's obsession with sex makes him a natural target for *oni* and related creatures. The related creatures turn out to be the gods, Shinto, Buddhist, and otherwise. The difference between these gods and the *oni* is debatable. In one episode, Lum's former classmates gather for a reunion. These include some other *oni* like Rei and Oyuki, but also the goddess Benten and a wide variety of other creatures. The blurred distinction between gods and demons is even more evident in another episode where Lum drags Ataru up to the Heavens to play on the *oni* team in their annual basketball game with the gods. At first the sides seem clear. The *oni*, all clad in tiger skins are a rowdy, abusive bunch, and just in case anyone had any doubts, they carry a banner marked "*oni*." The other side also carries a banner identifying them as gods. They need to. Except for the fact that they don't wear tiger skins, the gods are indistinguishable from the *oni*, being an equally loutish pack, determined to win at any cost. And, when Ataru messes up the game, both sides show equal levels of sadism in exacting their revenge.

Distinguishing the gods from the demons in Shinto and in *anime* is often difficult. One reason for this is that the gods are often so far from perfect. Another reason is that the demons are often less than purely demonic. Some are downright sympathetic. That is somewhat evident in a series like **Vampire Princess Miyu** which openly admits there's no real difference between gods and demons. The distinction is even more blurred in **Ogre Slayer**, a series which deals exclusively with *oni*.[16]

[14]Beef bowls are a favorite form of fast food in Japan. A mixture of seasoned beef and onions is served over a bowl of steaming hot rice. Many people add a raw egg mixed with a little soy sauce which cooks when it hits the rice. Rei's craving for beef bowls is roughly analogous to Wimpy's craving for hamburgers in **Popeye**.

[15]A *sakura* is a kind of cherry. **Urusei Yatsura** is a long string of puns, most of which are genuinely funny in Japanese. They lose much of their flavor in translation.

[16]There is a long debate regarding whether *oni* should be translated as "demon" or "ogre." In fact, Japanese folklore is sufficiently varied that this is really a matter of choice. An *oni* is an *oni*, either way.

The premise of **Ogre Slayer** is drawn from one of the darkest nightmares of Shinto folklore, the story of Katako or Kozuna, a young man who is half human, half *oni*. As such, he has the kindness of a human being and the strength of an *oni*. He uses his powers to kill other *oni* and to protect humans from them. As he grows older, however, his *oni* nature reasserts itself and he develops an urge to eat people. In some variations of the story, he simply recognizes the fact that he can no longer exist in the world of men and returns to the realm of the *oni*. In other versions, he begs to be killed before he can satisfy his growing appetite, or commits suicide by locking himself in a thatched hut and setting it alight. In all versions, he receives no reward at all for having tried to be good or for the lives he has saved.

In Kei Kunosuke's version, the **Ogre Slayer** is nameless. His mother was an ogre (*oni*), and although he takes the form of a young man, he is really an ogre himself. Instead of a horn, he was born with a sword strong enough to cut through ogre flesh and bone. He believes that if he uses the sword to kill all the ogres in the world, he will receive a name and become a human being. To that end, he travels throughout Japan saving people from ogres and killing off their attackers with a gentleness that reflects his own origins and, perhaps, an awareness that someday he, too, will need to be destroyed.

In **Ogre Slayer**, Kunosuke introduces her own theory concerning the origins of ogres. She is free to do so since Shinto mythology is vague on the subject. According to some myths, *oni* were created to torment souls in Hell and did not arrive in Japan until after the introduction of Buddhism. Other myths suggest that they are created when rites of purification after childbirth (a major source of pollution in Shinto terms because of the blood) are not properly observed. In **Ogre Slayer**, most ogres are born from the corpses of human beings, a theme consistent with Shinto ideas about impurity and corpses. (Kunosuke actually invokes this theme more forcefully in **Yoma: Curse of the Undead** when she posits a separate universe of evil born from the blood-soaked earth of the battlefields of Japan during the warlord era.) However, there are other means by which ogres come into the world, most of them having to do with women's issues. Some ogres are born to women who have been raped by ogres. Some are born of the loneliness of unpopular, unattractive women who are tormented for their misfortune. Some are the dearly loved children of female ogres. Some are called up by the rage of rape victims who are neither believed nor avenged. And then there are the many frustrated, outraged, angry women who become ogres themselves.

Like many *anime*, **Ogre Slayer** changes perspective from time to time so that the viewer sees the situation from the point of view of the ogres as well as their victims or their slayer. In one episode, for example, a child-eating *oni* is revealed to be the spirit of a noblewoman who went mad after her own child was devoured by another *oni* centuries before. Her transformation into an *oni* is more the result of grief than evil. Such changes of perspective combined with the Shinto view of an amoral universe makes it hard to tell the good guys from the bad, even when one side is composed of vicious, people-eating ogres.

Devilman goes one step further. The central character embodies both sides. He is Akira, and he begins the series as an exceptionally gentle, loving, and virtuous young man. Realizing that the Earth is in danger from a demonic invasion, he deliberately merges physically and emotionally with a demon to become Devilman. The theory is that because his original personality was so exceptionally good, he will be able to dominate and control the demonic half, while still retaining its powers to fight other demons. And so it works out, although his control is often less than complete, and his human persona definitely changes for the worse as he becomes increasingly insolent, arrogant, and abusive toward his girlfriend.

The concept of **Devilman** is supposedly drawn from the Judeo-Christian tradition. At any rate, there are periodic references to Dante's *Inferno*. Actually, **Devilman** owes more to the creative talents of its creator, Go Nagai, than to any religious or cultural source. The whole idea of uniting with evil in order to combat it is alien to Christian ideology. It's not so alien to Shinto, although using a captive demon as a protector the way Chiaki does in **Zenki** is more traditional. Moreover, Nagai's vision of Hell is not drawn from Shinto mythology, nor from Christian, Buddhist, or Taoist doctrines. Rather, it is a dreadful inversion of Darwinism, a primeval place where creatures evolve by devouring one another in order to acquire one another's strengths.

Devilman's demons are a bit more in the usual Japanese tradition. Even the worst of them have their redeeming features. For example, Shirenu, the bird woman who almost tears **Devilman** to shreds with her claws, turns out to have a lover, another demon who offers his own life so that she can have a meaningful death. She at first refuses. She is not only loved, but capable of loving in return. Her lover insists, stating that his life would have no meaning without her anyway. She then accepts his offer and the lovers die together, monstrous and evil no doubt, but true lovers just the same.

The Crystal Triangle shows a similar reluctance to take sides in the three-way contest between humanity, gods, and demons. In this Indiana Jones–style science fiction film, a Japanese archeologist searches for Jehovah's last message of hope for humanity which, as it turns out, was left in the care of Himiko, Japan's ancient shaman queen. (She turns up in a lot of *anime*.) He is assisted in his search by an old-fashioned young woman named Miyabe who knows more about Himiko than any living human could possibly know. That's because Miyabe is Himiko, something the audience realizes sooner than the love-struck archeologist. She has kept herself young all these years in a supernatural womb of her own creation. In it, she has grown old thousands of times, each time emerging snake-like from her old woman's body to swim young and fresh in her own amniotic fluid.

Miyabe/Himiko's assistance is of questionable value, however. She means well, but there is more than a little doubt about the good will of the gods she serves. True to the shamanistic tradition, Miyabe/Himiko serves as a channeler, allowing the gods to speak to humanity through her mouth. Throughout most of the movie, the beings who speak through her are the Hih, an alien race of monsters awaiting humanity's demise so that they can colonize the planet. In the end, Miyabe/Himiko sacrifices her life so that she can enter Jehovah's spaceship and transmit the final message. It is received by her heartbroken lover, the archeologist who thinks his worst problem is persuading humanity to accept it. The audience knows better. "Jehovah" was a green caterpillar who looked remarkably like an embryonic Hih. Humanity just might be better off without his message.

When the monstrous Hih take human form, they become remarkably ugly Buddhist monks. Indeed, Buddhist monks often play a negative role in *anime*. That often surprises American *otaku*. After all, Japan is a Buddhist country, isn't it? It is, but the main contact most Japanese have with Buddhism is when they must hire a priest to officiate at a funeral. Just as Shinto is the religion of life, of births, and of weddings, Buddhism is the religion of death. That doesn't mean the Japanese hate Buddhism. Death must be dealt with, after all. But it does mean that the religion has a distinctly somber image.

In recent years, Buddhist institutions have also developed a somewhat sleazy image. This is partly the result of some highly publicized scandals involving the financial misdeeds of some major sects. However, it is also the result of the fact that most Japanese tend to turn to Buddhism only in times of need. That need is most commonly the need to bury a relative, but there are others. In times of sickness, for example, Japanese may ask help from a monastery devoted to Yakushi, the Buddha of healing. In times of stress, they may have recourse to a Zen retreat. Or, they may simply choose to strengthen family ties by spending a vacation at one of the more hospitable monasteries which are often little different from Japanese style luxury hotels. In all these cases, although Buddhism undoubtedly provides something of value, it charges for the service. Sometimes it charges a lot, and the services provided are often poorly explained. Indeed, mystery is often part of the package. As a result, many Japanese come away feeling somehow "conned" even when the results are satisfactory. Even those who are deeply committed to the religion itself sometimes express doubts about the integrity of Buddhist institutions and professionals (monks, nuns, and priests). So, it's not too surprising that when an esoteric Buddhist sect challenges Ayaka Kisaragi for the Tokyo ghost-busting market in **Phantom Quest Corp.,** it turns out to be not only in league with demons, but greedy and criminal besides.

Things can get worse for Buddhism in *anime* where monks and priests are more likely to turn into demons than almost anyone else. In **Zenki**, the story of Chiaki, a schoolgirl Shinto priestess who controls a demon lord to protect her village from the evil goddess Karma,[17] Buddhist monks are cast as the opposition. Not only does the local temple use unethical tactics to lure tourists away from the heroine's bed and breakfast Shinto shrine, but sinister Buddhist pilgrims in the service of Queen Karma start the mayhem by breaking a seal while trying to rob her shrine of what they think is a treasure. Most of the monks or priests in **Zenki** are also greedy and/or lecherous, leaving them wide open to demonic possession in a variety of grisly forms. When **Zenki** is awakened, his first snack is a two-headed, demonic Buddhist pilgrim. Later on, a novice monk becomes a spider-like monster who preys on young women, storing them away in his web. Insects often seem to be connected to Buddhism. **Yoma: Curse of the Undead** also features a grim Buddhist priest who turns into an enormous, carnivorous spider. And the extraterrestrial priests in **The Crystal Triangle** assume insect-like forms.

[17]*Karma* is a Buddhist term which refers to the effects of one's actions on one's later life or future lives. It is not usually portrayed as a person.

Actually, **The Crystal Triangle** goes much further. It names the source of the evil that threatens to destroy the earth. The leader of the Hih, it turns out, was Kukai, the founder of the Shingon sect of Buddhism. In fact, Kukai was a ninth-century monk who traveled to

China, brought Shingon to Japan, founded the Mount Koya monastery, and lived a saintly life devoted to study, meditation, and charity. So, how did he wind up as the leader of a bunch of bug-eyed monsters in a science fiction *anime*?

Don't bother looking into the precepts of Shingon or Kukai's own writings. They speak of salvation and the infinite mercy of the Buddha. To understand why such a religion might be associated with demons and monsters, it's necessary to refer to the small traditions, the folk stories that surround individual Shingon temples. Better yet would be to go to the temples themselves. Start with Mount Koya. Stay in one of its many monastic hostelries. Walk the grounds. They're spooky. Mount Koya is one of the oldest and largest cemeteries in Japan. Located high on a mountain, it is a place of fog and damp. Moss drapes the ancient headstones and the looming pine trees. Ancient temples, well-maintained but obviously old, dot the paths. Inside those temples are statues that often look more Hindu than Buddhist with their many heads and angry, snarling faces. Even the gentler expressions of the seated figures on faded, ancient *mandalas* seem withdrawn and mysterious. Attend a service. Shingon services are elaborate affairs conducted before elaborate golden altars with more bells and smells than even the highest Catholic church. Don't expect to understand much of it. Nobody does, not even the Japanese.

Shingon is an off-shoot of Tantric Buddhism[18] which developed in Northern India and Tibet. There's nothing evil about it, but it has an overlay of magical elements and heroic legends modeled on Hindu myths that differentiates it from the usual simplicity of Japanese Buddhism. The focus of Shingon meditation, for example, is the *mandala,* a picture or design used to guide the believer's mind along the path to salvation. There's nothing magical about that, but over the years, the *mandala* itself has come to be regarded as a kind of talisman. Tantrism also uses chants of nonsense syllables in its meditative practices, and over the years these have become magical phrases. "On batari ya sawaka," the phrase with which **Tokyo Babylon**'s Sumeragi Subaru ends most of his incantations, is drawn from Tantric practices. "On" is usually written in English as "Aum" or "Ohm." "Sawaka" is simply the Japanese pronunciation of "savika." That's Sanskrit for "amen." **Zenki**'s Chiaki identifies herself as a Shinto priestess, but her divination chants are pure Tantrism. No wonder the subtitles don't try to translate it. It has roughly the same

[18]The feature of Tantric Buddhism best known to Americans is that some sects advocate meditation during the act of sex. Somehow this doesn't make its way into *anime* much which is odd. Think of the fun you can have with that one!

53

meaning as "Abracadabra," although admittedly it does sound a great deal more impressive

And its intent is benign. That, too, is not unusual. In both *The Crystal Triangle* and *Zenki*, Buddhism is salvation as well as threat. The alien Hih may take the forms of Buddhist monks and hole up in a mountain temple, but Kamishiro, the archeologist who opposes them, is also a devout Buddhist. Indeed, he was trained in Tibet and on several occasions he uses the Tantric practices he learned there to hold the Hih at bay. Similarly, *Zenki*'s Chiaki uses Tantric chants in her divinations and exorcisms. Significantly, neither Chiaki nor Kamishiro are Buddhist professionals. The mistrust of Buddhism seems to be confined to Buddhist practitioners and institutions. It has little to do with the religion itself.

That mistrust of religious institutions is also evident in science fiction where no real religion is involved. In *The Wings of Honneamise,* an early funeral scene establishes the orthodox religion of its fictional world as a superficial thing, and provides an explanation for why the hero is so drawn to Riquinni's simpler, more personal faith. *Green Legend Ran* provides a bitter burlesque of virtually all organized religions with the Rodoists, a despotic mix of religion and politics. Its bishops are deformed, lecherous creatures without much faith in the religion they supposedly represent. All they care about is power. In *Green Legend Ran,* even the simpler faith of young Aira turns out to be misplaced.

Even when Buddhism is on the side of truth and justice, its image remains grim. In *Judge,* for example, the Buddhist courts of Hell offer justice to those who can find none on earth. *Judge* is based on a well-known Buddhist legend, that of Lord Enma who judges the dead to determine the length of their stay in Hell. (The Buddhist Hell is as terrible as the Christian one, but at least it's not eternal.) Lord Enma is no Buddhist version of Satan. He is in no way evil. Judging souls is simply his job. However, he is one of Buddhism's sterner deities. And just in case Lord Enma alone isn't frightening enough, the creators of *Judge* have drawn on Chinese legends to give him nine companions, so that the accused must face ten kings of Hell. The accused is not terribly sympathetic. He is a successful businessman who murdered his best friend out of jealousy and greed. He deserves to stand trembling on Lord Enma's *mandala* of justice. However, when his victim is summoned to testify, he too rises from Hell, a pathetic wraith who can only whine that hadn't been ready for death. Yet, by all accounts the victim was a loving family man with a reputation for honesty in his personal and business dealings. If he had other failings, we are not told of them. The implication is that no one is blameless enough to avoid Lord Enma's court.

The most sympathetic Buddhist deity in Japanese legend and in *anime* is Kannon,[19] the goddess of mercy. Like many Buddhist gods, she is a *Bodhisattva,* a person who gained admission to Nirvana (paradise) through meditation, but who has remained on Earth to help those who are too weak to achieve salvation through their own efforts. Kannon is also closely associated with sex and with stripping. Indeed, the expression "going to see Kannon" means that one is going to watch a strip show. What does salvation have to do with stripping? Originally, nothing. This is a case of Buddhism and Shinto merging. Somehow, when Buddhism first came to Japan, Kannon became associated with Uzume, the Shinto goddess whose dance lured the Sun Goddess from her cave. Now she combines an image of unconditional, almost motherly love with unbridled eroticism. Small wonder she's so popular.

Mercy and sex are a powerful combination. That becomes apparent in Kannon's most effective *anime* appearance in the finale of **Doomed Megalopolis**. In **Doomed Megalopolis**, 1920s Tokyo is menaced by a powerful demon named Kato. Many mediums and priests try and fail to exorcize Kato. Finally a *miko,* a Shinto priestess, named Keiko takes on the job. Whether she becomes Kannon through shamanistic possession or has always been the goddess in disguise is unclear. However, she is certainly Kannon when she rides into the demon's stronghold, dressed in her Shinto robes, sword in hand, astride a ghostly white stallion. Kato is delighted to see her at first and attempts to rape her psychically with his army of hungry ghosts, crawling shadows that tear off her clothes and insert themselves into every orifice. Kannon quells them with a single gentle smile. Warmed by her gaze, the ghosts briefly return to their human forms. Then, glowing golden with her light, they ascend to paradise. The ghosts disposed of, Kannon turns her attention to the demon. Ripping off the last of her tattered robes, she advances on him offering him the one thing that will end his evil forever: absolute, unconditional, and unplatonic love. Unlike many *anime* depictions of naked women, this presentation of Kannon is no girlish, airbrushed male fantasy. Although slender, she is very much a mature woman with wide, angular hips and

[19]Some temples depict Kannon as male, others as female. In popular practice and in *anime*, however, Kannon is almost always a woman. Kannon is also the goddess to whom Japanese women bring their *mizuko* (water children), stone statues representing the souls of aborted fetuses. It's hard to imagine women bringing such an intimately female practice to a male deity.

heavy breasts. Her aggressive sexuality terrifies the demon, but eventually he succumbs to her embrace. As they join together, a pillar of golden light shoots up to the Heavens and Tokyo is saved yet again.

Kannon often shares altar space with another goddess, Benten. Like Kannon, Benten's unique attributes result from the combination of an alien goddess with a Shinto deity. The original Benten was the Taoist goddess of beauty, the arts, and fertility. Taoism in its popular form is the folk religion of China.[20] The early Japanese did not, apparently, find it as attractive as Buddhism, probably because it was too much like what they already practiced with Shinto. However, they did adopt Taoism's fortune-telling techniques and a few Taoist deities including Benten. In the original Taoist mythology, Benten was the only female among the seven Taoist gods of luck. She played the *biwa,* a stringed instrument much like a lute, and symbolized the womanly arts. All of the womanly arts, apparently. She set sail aboard the Treasure Ship (*takara-bune*) with six male companions[21] on a long and difficult trip. Such were her skills, that all six arrived in good humor with no complaints about the hardships they had undergone. According to Japanese folklore, the Seven Gods of Luck still come to port every New Year's Eve. Children who put a picture of them and their Treasure Ship beneath their pillows on that night will receive a lucky dream.

In Japan, Benten, like Kannon, became associated with a Shinto counterpart, Ryūgū Otohime, the Princess of the Dragon Palace, and a powerful goddess of the sea. Ryūgū Otohime, is the female protagonist in the story of Urashima Tarō, one of Japan's most popular folk tales and possibly the world's first tale of time as a dimension. Urashima Tarō was a young fisherman who rescued a turtle that was caught in his net. To reward him, the turtle took him beneath the sea to the Dragon Palace where he lived in luxury and became the princess's lover. After three years, he returned home for a visit. Before he left, the princess gave him a box with strict instructions not to open it. When he returned home, he found that time had passed more quickly there and everyone he had known was long dead. Despondent, he opened the box which, he discovered as he turned suddenly old, contained his

[20] In its scholarly form, Taoism is a sophisticated philosophy that should not be confused with these folk beliefs.

[21] The six other gods are: (1) Hotei, the fat, laughing god of happiness, (2) Jurojin, the elderly god of longevity, (3) Fukurokujin, the dwarfish god of wisdom, (4) Bishamon, the armor-clad god of religious zeal, (5) Daikoku, the smiling, generous god of wealth, and (6) Ebisu, the god of honest labor with his fishing pole in one hand and his catch, a fat *tai* (sea bream) in the other. Americans are most likely to be familiar with Hotei and Ebisu. The Chinese depiction of fat, laughing Hotei surrounded by children is often sold in Chinatown bric-a-brac stores. Ebisu appears on the label of Ebisu beer, a Japanese brew available in the U.S.

youth. It's hard to find a moral in this story, unless it's that mortals shouldn't mess with gods no matter how beautiful and well intentioned they may be. Ryūgū Otohime may well have loved Urashima Tarō, but she also destroyed him.

When Benten, the Taoist goddess of beauty, fertility, and the womanly arts became identified with Ryūgū Otohime, she added two new traits: the sea and an interest in romance as well as sex. In Japan, Benten is often portrayed as a white dragon and has been known to save children and sailors from less benevolent dragons. She is also the goddess of romance and often helps star-crossed lovers.

Rumiko Takahashi clearly has a special fondness for Benten who makes cameo appearances in both **Urusei Yatsura** and **Ranma ¹/₂** . In both cases, her sexy playfulness is at the core of her personality. In **Urusei Yatsura**, she is portrayed as a biker babe, sporting a variety of leather bikinis and hung with chains. The other lucky gods are also represented as biker types. Later in the series, it turns out that they all have daughters who sometimes join with Benten to form an all-female pack. Despite her appearance, Benten is one of the less lethal females in **Urusei Yatsura**. She is Lum's best friend and although she sometimes flirts with Ataru, she has no serious intention of challenging Lum's claim to him.

Benten and the seven lucky gods also make an appearance in the first Ranma movie: **Trouble in Nekonron, China.** For reasons of plot, the gods' names have been changed and so have some of their characteristics. Benten has been renamed Monlon, but otherwise she is far more recognizable as the original goddess than the biker babe in **Urusei Yatsura**. Although both versions have sex appeal, Monlon is infinitely more feminine. She sports flowing Chinese robes and plays the traditional *biwa*. Of course, she also uses her *biwa* strings in a bizarre form of martial arts. Now, that wasn't part of the original story.

The same influx of Chinese culture that brought Benten and the other lucky gods to Japan in the sixth century also brought the ideas of Confucianism. Few of these really caught on, and even those that did were so changed by the Japanese that few Chinese today would recognize them. However, Confucianism did add one new element to the world of Japanese folklore: the hungry ghost. Hungry ghosts are closely linked to Confucian ideas about filial piety and the need to honor one's ancestors even after death. In both China and Japan, people regularly honor the dead in their families by visiting their graves with gifts of food and alcohol.

But what happens to those who die without relatives to bring them goodies? They become hungry ghosts, forever doomed to walk the Earth hungry and alone. They are pathetic creatures, but they can also be terrifying. In Chinese mythology, hungry ghosts are often self-motivated and prey on those who were responsible for their having died alone and friendless. They can often be pacified by offerings made to their restless spirits. In Japan, however, they are at once more and less fearful. They seem to have little volition of their own. Rather, they are there to be used by other demonic forces.

That is certainly the case with the hungry shadows controlled by the demon Kato in **Doomed Megalopolis**. According to the plot, they are the ghosts of those who were buried alive as human sacrifices to the dragon who dwells in the Earth below Tokyo. (This is pure fiction. There are no records of any such sacrifices, although the dragon-in-the-Earth business comes from Taoist ideas regarding earthquakes.) Kato has organized these hungry ghosts and uses them as an army to work his will. Actually, Kato is something of a hungry ghost himself. He too died unmourned as a soldier in the Russo-Japanese War (1904–1905), and was buried without proper rites. In his case, however, other demonic forces have combined to make him a full-fledged demon rather than simply another hungry ghost.

Hungry ghosts can also be used by a human being, although this is risky and the user may become the used. Such is the case in **The Laughing Target**, a Rumik World offering which features a demonic schoolgirl named Azusa who is determined to rid herself of a rival in love by whatever means possible. Azusa grew up in a remote part of Japan and, unbeknownst to the relatives who take her in after her mother dies, has been the willing tool of hungry ghosts for years. Azusa's ghosts actually serve her rather well. Twice they save her from rape attempts by lending her supernatural strength and then by devouring the would-be rapists, thus avoiding police inquiries. However, each time she accepts their assistance, their power over her grows. By the time she reaches Tokyo and attempts to reassert her rights to the boy she was betrothed to in childhood by eliminating the girlfriend he has acquired in the interim, she is as much controlled by her ghosts as in control of them. The result is a truly spooky creature who invites horror and pity simultaneously.

In general, *anime*'s use of Chinese (and occasionally Korean) myths and legends is natural and fairly accurate. Japan has borrowed extensively from both countries and is, itself, clearly a part of the East Asian cultural sphere. However, *otaku* need to be wary when *anime* strays outside East Asia. Contrary to the Western belief that Asia begins at the Danube, Asia is a large place and has several major culture groups within it. At the very minimum, the Middle East, Central Asia, South Asia, Southeast Asia, and East Asia represent five very different cultures. The Japanese don't necessarily understand any of them (except East Asia) any better than Americans do. And they are as likely to present an inaccurate, biased view of these cultures.

Otaku often miss this because they assume that as Asians, Japanese must understand and be sympathetic to all other Asian cultures. If World War II failed to prove the erroneousness of that assumption, *anime* certainly does. Japan may have adopted much of China's culture, but most Japanese today know little of the country itself. When Japanese travel abroad, they are more likely to go to Europe or the United States than to China or anywhere else in Asia. China remains an exotic unknown. It is no accident that the cursed spring that turns Ranma into a girl is located in China. Or that Kato, the demon of **Doomed Megalopolis** rises from the earth in Manchuria. Or that Pai, the three-eyed heroine of *3 X 3 Eyes,* comes from there. In the eyes of many Japanese, China is still a place where anything could happen, and in *anime*, it usually does happen.

Hong Kong, in particular, is a place not only of mystery, but of crime and violence as well. The illegal genetic experiments that create **Genocyber** take place in Hong Kong. It is in Hong Kong that Pai and her comrades face down demons and gangsters in their efforts to find the statue of humanity that will make Pai human and restore Yakumo's life. Hong Kong is also the base for the criminal organization that makes an assassin of a gifted potter in **Crying Freeman**. To be fair, most of this image is drawn from Hong Kong's own movie industry. Hong Kong's movies, particularly its *kung-fu* and horror movies are extremely popular in Japan. However, the image remains despite the fact that Hong Kong is a popular destination for Japanese tourists, especially young people on a budget.

The use of Chinese mythology in *anime* is also much more rough and ready than the use of Japanese traditions. Most of the Shinto adaptations in *anime* are at least partly based on some reality, and even the changes reveal a deep understanding of the original. That is certainly not the case in *anime* like, for example, **Dragon Ball. Dragon Ball** is supposed to be based on a sixteenth-century Chinese novel, *Monkey: A Journey to the West.* The original novel is an interesting mix of social satire, religious commentary, and adventure fiction. As Monkey and his two companions, Sandy and Pigsy, travel to the West (in this case, India) in search of Buddhist scriptures, they meet with a variety of gods and demons and learn spiritual truths from each experience. More popular versions produced by Chinese opera troupes added acrobatics and slapstick humor to the story, but they didn't change the basic plot. In **Dragon Ball**, one of the characters, Goku, does sport a monkey tail, and another, Oolong, is portrayed as a pig in a Mao jacket. The quest theme remains although instead of Buddhist scriptures, the goal is now a set of golden dragon balls which, if assembled, will grant the owner a wish. That does not make **Dragon Ball** an adaptation of *Monkey*. It's not just that new characters have been added or that the adventure soon turns into science fiction, the entire spirit of the original is lost. As a novel, *Monkey* was often funny, but its humor was not based on farting and it certainly contained no female characters named after gym shorts. (Bulma, in Japanese, is written as *buruma,* bloomers.) That doesn't mean **Dragon Ball** is without value. It's perfectly good kiddie *anime*. It just has nothing to do with the Chinese novel.

Things get even stranger when *anime* leaves East Asia. The Middle East, India, and Southeast Asia are as foreign to the Japanese as they are to Americans, and most Americans will recognize *anime*'s images. The Middle East suffers the most from *anime* stereotyping. In *anime* such as **The Crystal Triangle, Area 88,** and even **GoShogun: The Time Étranger,** the Middle East is portrayed as a place of sand, religious fanaticism, and terrorists. It's a good place to go if you want to be killed. Southeast Asia isn't much better. **Patlabor II, Genocyber,** and **The Crystal Triangle** all feature scenes drawn from news reports of the Vietnam war. Beautiful beaches and lush tropical vegetation are overshadowed by menacing helicopters with guns at the ready. India seldom appears as a modern nation. If it appears at all, it remains a land of bejewelled rajas, yogis in mountain caves, or a source of exotic new martial arts techniques.

The rest of the world doesn't do too well in *anime* either. Africa is still fairly savage and mysterious. When the creators of **GoShogun: The Time Étranger** needed a death city, they drew narrow streets lined with Moroccan-style buildings and populated with dark-skinned, robed, fanatical inhabitants. Latin America is a den of drug dealers and terrorists in *anime*, a good place to send someone if you want them killed, as the villain of **Judge** does. America doesn't come off too well either. It's a place of crime, gangs, and racial tensions, a place where an

African American boy with psychic powers might become a crime boss before reaching puberty, as Sonny Lynx does in **Harmagedon.** Even Hawaii, a popular tourist spot for young Japanese, has its problems. No one is terribly surprised when **Kimagure Orange Road's** Hikaru gets kidnaped from her Waikiki hotel room. Hawaii, after all, is part of the United States. Europe does better, except in World War II movies when it becomes a land of ruins, prostitutes, and Nazis. At other times, however, Europe is still a never-never land of snowcapped mountains, castles, and knights in shining armor. Or even knights in race cars. Even in contemporary Europe, Lupin III manages to find a princess to rescue in **The Castle of Caliostro.**

Considering all that, it's not surprising to discover that *anime* doesn't do as well with alien mythologies. Incorporating elements of other mythologies into *anime* that have an essentially Japanese basis like **Silent Möbius** or **The Crystal Triangle** is one thing. Using an alien mythology as the basis for an *anime* generally results in either a bad *anime* or one in which the alien elements become Japanized.

The latter is the case in **Oh, My Goddess!,** a romantic comedy about a shy college student named Keiichi and the Norse goddess he accidentally summons while trying to order take-out noodles. Kosuke Fujishima, the creator of **Oh, My Goddess!,** clearly did his homework. Allowing for the vagaries of Japanese pronunciation, he has the names right. The goddess who falls in love with Keiichi is Belldandy, or rather, Verthandi, the Norn who symbolizes existence. She is soon joined by her two sisters, Urd (fate) and Skuld (necessity). Of course, Fujishima has changed their symbolism. In **Oh, My Goddess!,** Urd represents the past, Belldandy, the present, and Skuld, the future. But then, the original symbolism was pretty grim and not at all suitable for a romantic comedy. Neither were the original Norns. They controlled the destinies of humanity and cared for Yggdrasill, the great world tree which linked the different worlds and from which all things came. True, they occasionally took a young man under their wing, but that was usually to protect him in battle, not to cook and clean for him as Belldandy does for Keiichi.

Such changes can be chalked up to artistic license. If **The Crystal Triangle** can turn Queen Himiko into a starry-eyed schoolgirl, why shouldn't Fujishima turn Verthandi into a Japanese housewife? Yggdrasill has also changed into a cherry tree although it still links the different dimensions and is easily disturbed, something that causes real problems for Belldandy and Keiichi early in the series. The tree is also part of the universal computer net and has a small problem with bugs. These take the form of eight-legged rabbits. None has yet identified itself as Inaba, but that's probably just a matter of time. Even more surprisingly, all three goddesses feature Buddhist style "third eyes" in the center of their foreheads that light up whenever they perform some supernatural act. Now, they definitely didn't have that back home among the fjords!

In **Oh, My Goddess!**, Fujishima simply did with an alien culture what most Japanese animators do with their own. The result is inventive, playful, and well within the traditions of *anime* if not Norse mythology. The same is not true of *anime* like **The Heroic Legend of Arislan** or **Record of Lodoss War.** These *anime* draw their stock characters of elves, dwarves, wizards, and heroes from modern Western sources such as fantasy novels, sword and sorcery movies, and role-playing games. They are still based on Western mythology, but the interpretation is not Japanese. These *anime* reflect the way in which Western artists and authors have interpreted their own traditions. That doesn't make these movies bad. They are well made cartoons for adults, but they noticeably lack the delicate interplay of original myth and modern interpretation that is the hallmark of most good *anime*.

Things get really confusing when Japanese animators try to interpret Christian traditions. Fortunately, they don't try very often. Most *anime* presentations of Christianity go about as deep as Japanese "Christian" weddings. The bride may wear white as she walks down the aisle and the man who officiates may wear a dog collar. But a closer examination will reveal that the "chapel" in which the wedding takes place is simply a theatrical set attached to the hotel that will cater the wedding banquet. No services have ever been held there. There is no priest. The man in the dog collar is an actor. It's just that these "Christian" weddings are so much showier than traditional Shinto ceremonies. And most young Japanese women love that white dress!

And most *anime* depictions of Christianity are equally superficial and focused on image. **Hundred Pound Gospel,** for example, features a nun whose main connection to any religion seems to be her outfit. Costuming is also the main reason that **Tokyo Babylon's** hero, Sumeragi Subaru, sports outlandish outfits with crucifixes prominently displayed. It's not because he's Christian, it's because he's connected to the occult. The same is true of the supernatural defense attorney in **Judge.** His affinity for churches and for crossing himself is also a mark of his profession. Ranka, the doll demon of **Vampire Princess Miyu** stores her grotesquely transformed victims in an abandoned church, but there is no other reference to Christianity in the episode. Similarly, when Makie, the Black World heroine of **Wicked City,** finally marries her human lover, she does so in a church with stained glass windows. Or is it one of those hotel-run chapels? Churches can also reflect doom. In the opening episodes of the **Captain Harlock** series, Harlock's young ward is tortured by being forced to clean an enormous church floor with a tiny brush. Eventually, she is driven too far and falls to her death from its steeple.

That image of Christianity may seem odd to many Americans, but it's really no different from the image American film makers try to create when they use sets involving multi-armed Hindu statues to indicate something dark and mysterious. They have nothing against Hinduism. They probably know nothing about it and, more importantly, neither does their audience. Those multi-armed statues help create a spooky atmosphere precisely because they do represent the exotic unknown. *Anime* treats Christianity, and Hinduism for that matter, in much the same way.

But don't judge too hastily. Japan has been a borrower of other cultures for centuries, and sometimes what looks like a garbled *anime* version of someone else's culture may actually be a reflection of how that culture has been Japanized centuries before *anime* was even a gleam in Osamu Tezuka's eye. This is the case with **RG Veda,** a tale of warring gods seemingly drawn from India's classic text, the *Rig Veda*. In the *anime* version, however, the sides seem to have been switched. **RG Veda's** villain is the god Taishakuten (his Indian name is Indra[22]), a beautiful but cruel demon, who has gained the throne of Heaven by betraying and finally murdering King Ashura, the rightful ruler. Now Ashura's daughter, a little girl with a big sword, has joined with other gods to destroy Taishakuten and restore harmony to heaven. In the original *Rig Veda,* Taishakuten was the heroic king who saved India by slaying the vicious demon Ashura.

No, CLAMP didn't get the story wrong by accident.[23] Not by design either. **RG Veda** is, more or less, based on the story as it came to Japan in the ninth century. The *Rig Veda* version is the Hindu version. But Hinduism never made it in Japan, at least not as Hinduism. Elements of Hinduism did enter Japan as Tantric or Shingon Buddhism. Tantric Buddhism, however, developed at a time

[22]The reason that names can change so dramatically is because of the way Indian culture made its way to Japan. It went first to China and Korea where it was translated into ideographic characters. The Japanese then applied their own very different rules of pronunciation to the texts.

[23]CLAMP is the name used by an Osaka-based group that produces *shōjo manga*.

when Hinduism and Buddhism were in conflict. The story that came to Japan via Buddhist monks was a Hindu story adapted and told by the enemy. Naturally the gods became demons and vice versa.

In fact, a fair number of Hindu deities made their way into *anime* in their Buddhist forms. The fact is that Tantric Buddhism has provided Japan with a whole new set of stories about gods and demons, heroes and villains. Shingon, the most widespread form of Tantrism in Japan, features a large number of *Bodhisattva,* saints endowed with special powers who serve as the defenders of the faith. The number of those defenders varies from sect to sect. The Sanjūsangendō temple in Kyoto features twenty-eight such defenders in the form of life-size statues. They guard one thousand statues of Kannon, the *Bodhisattva* of mercy, in a darkened hall heavy with the smell of incense. As befits their role as defenders, most are armed. Some feature physical oddities such as Ashura who has three heads or Karura (Garuda) who has a bird's face and wings. They are supposed to be the good guys, but their appearance is the stuff of nightmares.

And the stuff of good *anime.* Not all the characters in **RG Veda** are drawn from Shingon stories, but most are. In addition to the more familiar Japanese names used in **RG Veda,** most have Sanskrit names. Aside from Taishakuten and Ashura, there's Karura (Garuda), Kujaku (Mahamayuri Vidyarajni), Kendappa (Gandharva), and Yasha (Yaksa). Others are Chinese and Japanese additions to the pantheon of *Bodhisattva* who defend Buddhism. Protective dragons, for example, are represented in **RG Veda** by King Ryū whose name means dragon and who carries a dragon sword.

[24] A peahen spirit, to be specific. In Japan, he became a peacock. In either form, s/he removes all the hindrances and calamities afflicting humanity, just as a peahen/peacock eats poisonous plants and worms and turns them into nectar.

Of course, CLAMP has taken some liberties. That's the whole point when *anime* draws on mythology. Kujaku and Karura have both had sex changes. Actually, Kujaku has usually been depicted as male in Japan although in India he was a she.[24] CLAMP gets around this intercultural sex change by depicting Kujaku as a beautiful, somewhat androgynous young man. Karura is another matter. Even in Japan, she is always depicted as a man, albeit a man with a bird's head. The fact that she becomes an Amazon with a bird on her shoulder in **RG Veda** must be chalked up to CLAMP's artistic license. The same is true of the decision to portray Ryū as an adolescent.

Actually, Kujaku and Ashura often appear together in *anime* and *manga* although not in anything else that has yet reached the United States.[25] **RG Veda** may not be a good way to learn anything about the *Rig Veda,* but it's an excellent introduction to a little known aspect of Japanese folk Buddhism. There is almost no other way to learn about such folk beliefs, short of growing up in Japan. They are pervasive, but they have little if any textual basis.

All societies have such beliefs. In America, for example, horror films make extensive use of the legend of Lucifer and the fallen angels. Yet, a serious scholar of American religious practice would need to dig deep into medieval European history to find the basis for such beliefs. They do not exist in contemporary Christian scripture. That doesn't mean the belief doesn't exist in America. And the same is true in Japan, but because of it's long history of religious tolerance and its tendency to borrow freely from other cultures, Japan's treasure house of stories is larger and more varied than most. That is probably the real reason that *anime* has traveled so easily throughout the many cultures of East, Southeast, and South Asia. It's not just that the simple features of its characters allow a wide variety of people to see themselves, or that the basic mouth movements make dubbing easy. It's also that the stories, having been drawn from all of these cultures, are universal enough that everyone can find something that looks familiar.

The Western content of *anime* is small. Japan has not, after all, been in contact with the West for very long. And it remains to be seen whether Americans, Europeans, Africans, and Middle Easterners will find *anime* plots and themes as universal as most of Asia has already done. America, so far, has been the most receptive to *anime*, perhaps because it isn't really as fully Western in its culture as Europeans and many European Americans would like to think. America really is more like a salad bowl than a melting pot, and so is *anime*.

[25]At least, no other *anime* featuring Ashura and Kujaku have reached the United States. For those who can understand Japanese, **Kujaku-Ō** (King Kujaku) is an excellent series in which Ashura and Kujaku appear in present day incarnations to fight supernatural evils.

Chapter Four

Other Heroes, Other Villains

The crisis breaks out at least once a year. Some journalist new to the Tokyo Press Club comes across a novel, a movie, a video game or a *manga* in which a World War II soldier is portrayed as a hero. Then comes the news flash. Japanese fascism has once again reared its ugly head. The war drums are beating. Pearl Harbor should be on twenty-four hour alert. *Otaku* who know something about Japan generally just roll their eyeballs and let it go. Even *otaku* who know nothing about Japan realize there's something wrong with this argument even if they can't quite put their fingers on what it is.

That's because anyone who watches even an occasional *anime* soon learns that the Japanese definition of a war hero is subtly different from the American one. Americans like their heroics pure. It's not enough for our heroes to be brave and self-sacrificing. They must also have fought for a cause that was honest and pure and true. Winning helps, too. This definition of heroism causes Americans a lot of problems as they try to come to terms with veterans of the Vietnam war, which may be one reason why so many children of the Vietnam generation prefer the Japanese version.

The Japanese hero is defined by motivation. The ideal Japanese hero is not only brave and self-sacrificing, but selfless and unconcerned with personal gain or survival. The cause is not important. The hero's willingness to give his or her all to it is what counts. Winning doesn't matter either. In fact, it sometimes seems that the Japanese prefer a hero who loses. Losing and therefore gaining nothing confirms the hero's altruism and renders his or her sacrifice all the more tragic. As a result, it is quite possible to portray a young *kamikaze* pilot as a hero without necessarily endorsing the agenda of the Japanese fascists. Indeed, almost all Japanese portrayals of the war include very unflattering depictions of the leadership. World War II heroes are drawn from the ranks of the common man or woman who emerges from carnage with his or her ideals intact.

Of course, there aren't a lot of *anime* about World War II available in the United States. *Anime* distributors aren't completely crazy. Those that are available are tear jerkers like **Grave of the Fireflies** or **Barefoot Gen.** Both *anime* not only carry a pacifist message, but they see the war through the eyes of a child. That not only increases the pathos, but it allows the audience to bypass questions of ideology. That's probably more important for the Americans than it is for the Japanese.

Japanese audiences don't seem to mind heroes whose causes are less than admirable. One clear example of this is the popularity of the *shinsengumi*. The *shinsengumi* were a group of samurai who fought to defend Japan's old feudal order against the Westernizing forces that threatened to overthrow it in 1868. Fortunately, they did not succeed. The Westernizers had their way and Japan became a great power. If the *shinsengumi* had won, Japan could easily have wound up as a colony of Great Britain, and most Japanese know it. However, the fact that the cause itself was completely lame-brained is irrelevant. The point is that the young men who fought and died with the *shinsengumi* did so without any thought for their own self-interest, while those crafty Westernizers had a lot to gain from their revolution. As Hijikata Toshizo, a *shinsengumi* samurai torn out of time to live in the cloud world of **Zeguy,** admits to Miki, he can no longer really remember what he fought for. He still carries his old banner, but it reads simply "Truth" (*makoto*). He doesn't know what it is exactly, but he's willing to die for it. And Miki, a normal schoolgirl except for a few unexpected supernatural talents, is willing to adore him for that.

Anime actually contains few pure heroes and those who do appear consistently in that role tend to be supporting characters. They also don't talk much. There's a good reason for that. They have no personalities. **Zeguy**'s Hijikata, for example, is tall, dark, and handsome. He's brave, fights well, and believes in "Truth." That's pretty much all we ever learn about him. It may be enough for an adoring schoolgirl like Miki, but it's not enough for a discerning *anime* audience, accustomed to more complex characterizations. In **Zeguy,** the central character is not Hijikata, but Miki. She has her moments of heroism too, but she also has her moments of sheer human terror and doubt, like when she's being attacked by a demonic cyborg with half his face ripped off. She also has a sense of humor and sometimes changes her mind. Pure heroes can't afford to do any of that. Pure heroes, in fact, are pretty dull.

So are pure villains. That's not as immediately obvious since *anime* villains are very frequently nonhuman. In many *anime* they are demons or invading aliens. Either way, their nonhuman qualities give them a measure of interest they would not otherwise have. When they are human, however, the problem becomes clear. Villains are as predictable as heroes and defined by the same criteria. As heroes are altruistic and put other's interests before their own, so villains are motivated by self-interest and will sacrifice anyone else, including often their own loyal supporters, to get what they want. Such is the case with the villainous "Old Man in Hakone" who makes a brief appearance in **The Crystal Triangle**. As a cameo, his unadulterated hunger for power and his disdain for the lives of anyone other than himself, is chilling. The same is true of "the Old Man in Kamakura" in **Sohryūden** or the self-serving, ambitious bureaucrats in **Patlabor.** Such characters are never the center of attention, however. A little total evil goes a long way. In *anime* as in many other forms of fiction, drama is provided by those whose responses are less predictable.

Most *anime* heroes are only heroes some of the time. The same is true of many of the villains. Moreover, since character development and change is a major feature of *anime* series, it's not unknown for heroes to become villains and vice versa. And, since heroism is a matter of character and motivation, simply being on the right side doesn't guarantee anyone respect. For that matter, being a villain is not the same thing as being the enemy. In *anime*, the enemy is quite often an heroic figure. He's just a hero on the other side.

That definition of heroism is welcome to many young Americans who find it difficult to find a real cause to believe in. Like many young Japanese, they see themselves in a character like Shiro Lhadatt, the alienated hero of **The Wings of Honneamise. The Wings of Honneamise** is set in a kingdom on a planet that is Earthlike enough to be familiar without being clearly identifiable. In the same way, Shiro Lhadatt is identifiable more as a generation than a member of any particular nationality. He is a member of the Royal Space Force, a demoralized bunch of losers from whom no one expects much. Shiro searches for meaning in all the wrong places. He meets a young woman named Riquinni who claims to have found fulfillment in a new religion. It's not clear why Shiro is attracted to Riquinni, who is far from pretty, brusque in manner, and burdened with a singularly unappealing child. At first, it seems to be her faith that attracts him. It's not so much what she believes in, but that she is able to believe in something. Later, however, he almost destroys their fragile relationship when he tries to rape Riquinni. In the end, Shiro finds meaning in the conquest of space. Not in the Space Force itself. He knows that to be corrupt and unreliable. Shiro finds meaning in the cold, clear purity of space itself and in the purity of his own commitment to it. That makes him very much a typical Japanese hero, but it also makes him an ideal hero for Generation X.

Most American *otaku* recognize that, but they can't always figure out exactly what it is about Japanese heroes that attracts them. The situation is further complicated by the fact that they seldom see the original models. Most of the heroes who appear in *anime* are based on legendary warriors from Japan's past. The original stories from which these heroes are drawn actually are often available in animated form, as historical *anime*. Unfortunately, few of them make it to America. Distributors generally consider them risky since most Americans have little or no knowledge of Japanese history. Some historical dramas do better than others.

The Dagger of Kamui, for example, deals with the Meiji Restoration of 1868, the overthrow of the old feudal government, and the beginning of Westernization. Aside from World War II, that is probably the event in Japanese history that some Americans are likely to have heard of. In any case, about half of **The Dagger of Kamui** takes place in America. Moreover, the political shenanigans that affect the hero's life have to do with the acquisition of Hokkaido, Japan's northernmost island. This is an obscure aspect of the Meiji Restoration and, since it is likely to be unfamiliar to Japanese as well, it is fairly well explained in the dialogue. Even more important is the fact that the hero, Jirō, is an Ainu, an ethnic minority from northern Japan. Ainu customs are different from Japanese customs, and so those too get explained in the script. That doesn't necessarily make **The Dagger of Kamui** popular. Many *otaku* complain that it's overly long and talky. But at least it's not hopelessly confusing.

The most common heroic ideal found in *anime* is drawn from a samurai ideal set down in the seventeenth century by samurai authors like Musashi Miyamoto who wrote *The Five Rings* or Tsunetome Yamamoto whose book *Hagakure* begins with the phrase "The way of the samurai is death." They called their ideal *"bushido,"* the way of the warrior, and extolled martial virtues such as loyalty to one's lord and one's comrades, stoic courage, and personal altruism. Most Americans and many Japanese regard *The Five Rings* and *Hagakure* as the original source on the subject of *bushido*. In fact, both books were written after the end of Japan's true warrior era. They were written during the Tokugawa era (1601–1868), an era in which the samurai class steadily lost their wealth, power, and prestige to a rising merchant class. They are nostalgic constructs created by samurai who felt lost and out of place in their seventeenth-century world of bustling cities and powerful merchants. They longed for a simpler world when right and wrong were clearly defined, a world where men were real men and women were real women. They longed for a past that never was.[1]

They based their ideas about samurai behavior on even older legends such as the story of Kusunoki Masashige, a fourteenth-century samurai who supported the cause of Emperor Godaigo. Godaigo, like all Japanese emperors, had no real power. He was a spiritual leader. The actual government was run by a Shogun who ruled in the emperor's name. In the 1330s, Godaigo tried to take advantage of the overthrow of one Shogunal family by another, and restore real power to the throne. Godaigo's cause was lost from the start, but that doesn't alter the heroism of his main general, Kusunoki Masashige who wound up committing *seppuku* in a farmhouse to avoid capture. Indeed, the fact that the cause was lost from

[1]Rumiko Takahashi has fun exposing the difference between theory and reality for Tokugawa samurai in an **Urusei Yatsura** episode where Musashi himself is revealed to be an expert, not on the way of the warrior, but on the way of running out on a restaurant bill.

the start only highlights the disinterested nature of Kusunoki's loyalty. In reality, Kusunoki's character and motivations were more than a little problematic, but by the seventeenth century his legend was secure with nostalgic samurai like Miyamoto or Yamamoto who learned their history more from ballads and Kabuki plays than from history books. They created an ideal from such legends, and they called their ideal *bushido*.

Later generations took that ideal literally. The Kabuki theater of the Tokugawa era alternatively praised and ridiculed *bushido*, but never doubted that it had existed. Propagandists of the 1930s and 1940s used it to persuade young men to give up their lives to Japanese imperialism. Later, author Yukio Mishima[2] used his talents to give it fresh life. On a less lofty level, the Japanese media continues to present idealized samurai heroes as part of Japan's daily fare. *Anime* presents its fair share.

[2]Mishima was a fine author, but a bit of a nut politically. In 1970 he committed ritual *seppuku* to protest modern Japan's decadence and to bring his own life in line with the values of the past as he perceived them.

Probably the best *anime* example of the *bushido* ideal available to Americans is **The Hakkenden,** a long saga of honor, destiny, and bloodshed set in the fifteenth century, just at the time when Japan's weakened central government gave way and warlord chaos overtook the country. Few Americans know much about this early era. Unfortunately, most Japanese do, so the creators of **The Hakkenden** felt no need to include much in the way of explanation. Actually, on one level, an ignorance of Japanese history may be an asset since the series introduces blatant anachronisms like the use of muskets and the practice of crucifixion. These did not reach Japan until almost a century later when the West arrived. That historical inaccuracy is the result of the fact that *Nanso Satomi Hakkenden,* the novel which inspired the *anime*, was also written during the Tokugawa era by yet another disgruntled, poverty-stricken samurai yearning for a past that had never existed except in his mind. He was an effective storyteller, but a poor historian.

Americans are also likely to be confused about the possible Christian significance of the crucifixion scene which occurs in **The Hakkenden.** A similar scene occurs in **Kabuto** which plays, more accurately, in the sixteenth century. In fact, such crucifixions are only distantly and indirectly related to Christianity. When the Westerners first arrived in the middle of the sixteenth century, they brought their religion with them. Unfortunately, the main thing Japan's warlords seemed to learn from the story of Christ was that crucifixion is a truly horrific way to kill someone. They used it frequently as a means of torture, execution, and terror. When Japan was reunited in 1601 and Christianity was banned, crucifixion remained in the new Shogun's judicial system as the ultimate form of capital punishment. Today, it remains linked in the minds of most Japanese with the brutality of feudal rule. It does not necessarily imply any reference to Christianity.

But crucifixion isn't the only thing American viewers may find odd about **The Hakkenden.** For all its flaws as an accurate historical account, **The Hakkenden** is an excellent portrayal of the same nostalgic ideal of samurai heroism made famous in America by *The Five Rings* and *Hagakure*. The heroes of **The Hakkenden** behave according to the code of *bushido*, the way of the warrior. The fact that there was no such thing as *bushido* in the fifteenth century (the term itself was invented later) is irrelevant. *Bushido*'s rules are as well known and understood by contemporary Japanese as if they had really existed.

At the core of *bushido* is loyalty to one's lord. That seems simple enough to preclude any attempt at dramatic tension. Good samurai will obey their lord. Bad samurai won't. It's not that simple and it never was, not even in the nostalgic reveries of poverty stricken samurai like Bakin Takizawa, the author of the novel on which **The Hakkenden** is based. Like most storytellers of his era, Takizawa loved to place his characters in positions where duty (*giri*) conflicted with personal feelings (*ninjō*). In **The Hakkenden,** Shino faces a classic *giri-ninjō* conflict when duty requires him to leave Hamaji, the girl he loves, in a dangerous situation so that he can fulfill his father's dying wish and his duty to his lord. Duty wins out, but that doesn't mean Shino feels any better when Hamaji disappears. He would have felt equally bad if he'd made the opposite choice. In a *giri-ninjō* conflict, there is no right answer except, perhaps, *seppuku*,[3] ritual suicide.

Seppuku is an intensely painful form of suicide by self-disembowelment. Its origin is unknown, but it seems likely that its original purpose was to avoid capture in battle and the possibility of revealing secrets under torture. The painful method eliminates all suggestions that the person who performs *seppuku* is taking the easy way out. *Seppuku* is an honorable alternative in any situation in which there is not other solution without dishonor. It is sometimes the solution to a *giri-ninjō* conflict, although when the *ninjō* involves romantic love, a gentler form of double suicide, often by drowning, is more usual.

Seppuku is more common in cases of conflicting loyalties, such as when two superiors issue conflicting orders. The Japanese feudal system was a complex hierarchy and most men had more than one lord above them. Moreover, the

[3]*Seppuku* is better known in the West as *harakiri*. This, however, is a derisive term (it means belly-slitting) and not suitable to the values of **The Hakkenden.** *Harakiri* also refers only to male *seppuku* which involves disembowelment. Women got a break where ritual suicide was concerned. Although the opening ceremonies were the same, female samurai preserved their modesty by driving the short sword into their throat rather than exposing their midriffs and entrails.

Confucian doctrines of filial and familial loyalties often conflicted with political loyalties. All of these factors come into play for Shino's father in *The Hakkenden* when Otsuka demands that he give up a sword entrusted to his care by his dying lord. That demand places Shino's father in an impossible position. Otsuka is the village elder and also the family head. As such, he is a type of "lord" and Shino's father owes him loyalty and obedience. Moreover, Otsuka is demanding the sword on behalf of his own lord. Shino's father, however, made a promise that binds his loyalties to the dead lord he once served and, more importantly, to the dead lord's son. If he refuses to hand over the sword, he has failed to show proper respect and loyalty to Otsuka, his immediate superior. Refusal also jeopardizes his family's safety. Yet, if he does hand it over, his personal honor is lost. Instead of doing either, he commits *seppuku*. By doing so, he bequeaths his son sufficient prestige to ensure that he will be able to keep the sword. This kind of *seppuku* is also a form of protest. It is the ultimate way of saying "look what you made me do."

Bushido was slightly different for samurai women. They, too, were expected to commit *seppuku* if their honor was compromised, but in their case, that honor was most often bound up in chastity. And they were not expected to disembowel themselves. That would have been immodest. Instead, they bound their limbs so that they would not fall in a compromising position and drove their short swords into their throats. This was pretty much the only advantage samurai women had over men. Although commoner women were fairly independent during the warlord era, samurai women were essentially marriage pawns.

That reality is reflected in the opening episode of *The Hakkenden* when the Lord of Awa promises his daughter to a dog if the mutt will bring him the head of his enemy. When the dog does so, he tries to welch on the deal. His daughter, however, will have none of it. "A promise is a promise," she tells her father. The truth is, she is in a double bind. Honor as defined by male standards, demands that she protect her father's word by marrying the pooch. However, honor defined as chastity, also demands that she not sleep with an animal. She does not commit *seppuku*. Actually, this would have been an honorable alternative, but then, of course, there would have been no novel. Instead, she goes to the mountains to live platonically with her dog husband. There, she faces another problem since the dog desires her. She keeps him at bay by assuring him that she will kill herself the moment he tries to assert his marital rights. Despite all these precautions, she unaccountably finds herself pregnant. A voice prophesies that she will bear a litter of eight noble warriors. Those, of course, are the eight dog warriors, the *"hakken"* of the title. Born, however spiritually, of a brave dog and an honorable woman, they represent the eight faces of honor: filial piety (*ko*), duty (*gi*), benevolence (*jin*), loyalty (*chū*), sincerity (*shin*), propriety (*rei*), wisdom (*chi*), and obedience (*tei*).

Those faces of honor go far beyond the relatively small genre of historical *anime*. The adventures of the eight dog warriors of **The Hakkenden** also follow a pattern familiar to most *otaku*. First, the characters are introduced. Next, they learn about each other. Tensions develop and are resolved as they recognize their mutual bond. By the end, they are a team, each member willing to sacrifice himself for the other and for the greater whole. The Star Force of **Star Blazers** go through the same process. So, for that matter, does the crew of the Starleaf in **Gall Force,** and the Knight Sabers in **Bubblegum Crisis/ Bubblegum Crash.** Modern Japanese women are less than enthusiastic about the submissive form of *bushido* epitomized by Princess Fuse. Most of them, faced with a dog for a husband, would call the SPCA. They prefer to see themselves in the male heroic model and have simply appropriated it. Female *otaku* in America tend to agree with this decision.

American *otaku* of both sexes tend to agree with the importance and dramatic impact of decisions involving honor both in its *giri-ninjō* form and in its discussion of conflicting duties. That seems odd. American society is not big on the idea of duty as an external force. Young Americans who face conflicts between their personal feelings and other loyalties or between alternate sources of authority are usually urged to look within, to examine their hearts, or to listen to their personal God. The inflexible dictates of *giri* should be not only alien, but downright unattractive to them. Yet that is not always the case. Many young Americans seem attracted to the idea of a moral code however harsh, that requires no further soul searching on their part.

And, they recognize the dramatic potential of such a code. Because of the dictates of absolute loyalty and duty, *anime* is able to indulge in a combination of unabashed sentimentality while still remaining unpredictable. The American media offers up a fair number of TV shows and movies that idealize friendship and romantic love, but these are painfully predictable. True lovers may die (although that's rare enough), but they will not betray their love. True friends may mess up occasionally, but in the end they come through for each other. Anyone who fails that test obviously wasn't a true friend or lover.

That's not true in a world where *giri* reigns supreme. **Star Blazers** already gave some hint of that when Captain Avatar (Okita) deserted his beloved family to follow his duty even when he knew that duty would lead to a lonely death far from home. Later in the *Yamato* series, *giri* played an even stronger role. In **Be Forever Yamato,** Susumu Kodai (Derek Wildstar) screamed as he was forced to abandon his beloved Yuki (Nova) to certain capture by sadistic aliens. But he left her all the same. *Giri* called. And much later, in **Final Yamato,** the young couple went out together in a blaze of *kamikaze* glory on the very eve of their long delayed wedding. The *Yamato* series may be set in the future, but its values are deeply rooted in Japan's past.

The same is true of another feature of *anime* that regularly puzzles Americans. That is the large number of effeminate male warriors. This, too, comes from the samurai tradition. The samurai, like the ancient Greeks, regarded same-sex relationships between men as a vital part of warrior training. In particular, relationships between an older samurai and the boy he was training were common. Actually, the ideal samurai stopped short of sleeping with his young ward. He loved from a distance, hopelessly, resolutely, and loyally. Samurai literature is filled with references to beautiful young men who were also fine swordsmen and fearless warriors. The Kabuki theater catered to samurai patrons by bringing such youths to the stage. Later, the all-female Takarazuka theater added to the tradition by having such roles played by women.

The model for all these beautiful, lethal young warriors was Yoshitsune Minamoto, a twelfth-century samurai who helped inaugurate samurai rule. Although small and girlish in appearance, Yoshitsune was a formidable warrior. In fact, his military skill made his older brother, Yoritomo Minamoto, Japan's first Shogun. Unfortunately, soon after their victory, the brothers became rivals. Given that his brother was the reigning Shogun, Yoshitsune never stood a chance. He headed for the hills accompanied by a few loyal followers. Finally, when he could run no further, Yoshitsune committed *seppuku* after first killing his wife and family to prevent them from falling into enemy hands. His loyal retainers held off the Shogun's forces to allow him time to make an honorable end. Most of them died with him.

Contemporary records do not credit Yoshitsune with any rare beauty. They simply state that he was surprisingly strong given how small and youthful he looked. That's hardly surprising. Yoshitsune became a warrior while still in his teens. He was barely thirty years old when he died. It was the nostalgia of the Tokugawa period (1601–1868), the same nostalgia that produced the romance of *bushido*, that really re-created Yoshitsune as a romantic figure with homoerotic overtones. The Kabuki theater in particular was fond of casting female impersonators (*onnagata*) to play Yoshitsune, a choice that guaranteed his "girlishness." Most plays dealt with the last days of his life, showing him as a helpless victim rather than the proud general he had once been. The male lead was left to Benkei, an enormously strong monk, who was one of Yoshitsune's most loyal retainers.

A similar fate befell Shiro Amakusa, a Christian samurai who led a peasant uprising in 1638. It was a hopeless cause and poorly planned. Amakusa and his followers were brutally massacred by Shogunal soldiers within the year. That wasn't surprising. Amakusa was only sixteen years old and thoroughly inexperienced. Some historians have suggested that he was merely a figurehead; others, that only an inexperienced child would ever have taken on such a hopeless cause. Whatever the truth, Amakusa soon became an underground hero symbolizing resistance to Shogunal rule. Later, in the 1960s he emerged again as a symbol of the underdog fighting oppression. In each case, his youthful, girlish appearance simply added luster to his legend.

The 1990s and *anime* have not been so kind to Amakusa. In **Samurai Showdown,** an *anime* based on a popular video game, he has been recast as the villain. Moreover, he has become a woman, an evil sorceress who deliberately betrayed her comrades for her own selfish reasons during the Shimabara uprising. The hero has become a villainess.

Indeed, the 1990s have not been kind to Japan's beautiful youth (*bishōnen*) tradition in general. This may be related to the importation of Western attitudes toward homosexuality and effeminacy. Beautiful, androgynous young men still abound in *anime*, but they are seldom warriors. When they are, they are usually vicious villains. This is certainly the case with Yorimaru of **Ninja Scroll**. He may speak softly, wear his hair in a boyish style and yearn after his evil overlord, but he's also the most dangerous of the eight demons of Kimon. He kills off one of his own allies, possibly because she was a sexual rival, and almost destroys the good guys. **Akai Hayate** introduces a more contemporary example of villainous androgyny in Genbu, the smirking, sweet-voiced, long-haired assassin who lies, murders, and steals in his efforts to take over the Shinogara ninja group and possibly the world. There's also

Chapter Four

Mr. J, the biologically enhanced psychic from FRAUD, who tries to destroy Ai and her father in *Ai City.* He's not exactly a villain; his loyalties are just unfortunate. But he's still a sinister figure with his soft voice, pretty face, and lethal intentions. Benten, the beautiful transvestite policeman of *CyberCity Oedo,* does a bit better. Within the time frame of the series, he is a policeman and on the right side of the law. But he wasn't always, and the few references to what he used to do sound distinctly unsavory.

Not all warrior types are drawn from the samurai model. There are other heroic traditions in Japan. Probably the best known to Americans are the *ninja. Ninja* are not samurai and never were. They were commoners who developed a martial arts technique, *ninjutsu,* and sold their services to the highest bidder. Their skills included more than just fighting techniques like the use of *shūriken,* throwing stars with sharpened, sometimes poisoned edges. Young ninja were schooled in the arts of disguise, camouflage, seduction, poisons, and breaking and entering. Sometimes the difference between a *ninja* and a common criminal was very small indeed. The heyday of the historical *ninja* was in the fifteenth and sixteenth centuries when warlords battled for the right to become the next shogun. The *ninja* served such warlords as spies, thieves, kidnappers, and assassins.

Their legend is a bit more romantic. *Ninja* are often credited with supernatural powers. They were thought to have the power to become invisible and to leap like monkeys from tree to tree. Often they were portrayed as shape-shifters. Some were credited with the ability to fly. A few even showed signs of samurai-like altruism, taking on worthy clients who would not be able to pay. As heroic ideals go, however, *ninja* send a mixed message at best.

Of necessity, *ninja* ideas about honor were different from those of the samurai. Loyalty was a shifting value to most *ninja.* Leaders of large *ninja* organizations like the Iga and Koga schools asked for, and sometimes got, loyalty from their followers. Many *ninja* also prided themselves on remaining absolutely loyal to a customer for as long as the job lasted. Of course, that meant that *ninja* could not afford any loyalty to one another, not when they might be employed by opposing sides the next day. Chastity as a form of honor was definitely out for female *ninja* and, indeed, for attractive young male *ninja.* Seduction ranked high as one of the arts of *ninjutsu.* In legend, and probably in reality, being a *ninja* was a lonely profession. Much of their popularity with present day audiences both in Japan and in the United States probably has to do with their ultimate, total alienation from society, an alienation that is only too familiar to the young of both countries.

That loneliness is best epitomized by the relationship between Marou and Hikage in **Yoma: Curse of the Undead.** The entire *anime* is a repudiation of the heroic legend of the samurai. The *yoma,* the ghost demons of the title, are created from the blood-soaked earth of sixteenth-century Japan's battlegrounds. The samurai are no honorable heroes; they are mere killing machines. The lone hero, such as he is, is a *ninja* who has been ordered to kill his best friend, a young samurai named Marou, a boy he grew up with. There are reasons. The official reason is that Marou betrayed the warlord they both serve. Later it transpires that Marou, who is distinctly girlish in appearance, has also sold his soul to the powers of darkness. He has become a demon, a cannibalistic ghoul. Hikage struggles valiantly to maintain some kind of honor amid all his shifting loyalties. He manages at least to remain human. By the end of **Yoma,** that alone is a triumph. Marou, who actually gets a second chance, shows no sign of doing so well.

Ninja Scroll also portrays the eerie world of the legendary *ninja*, but this time the setting is no longer the warlord era. Instead, **Ninja Scroll** takes place during the Tokugawa era, the same peaceful, prosperous era which produced the dream of *bushido*. But there's little sign of that in **Ninja Scroll** which is a fantasy with little historical basis. The main reality is that the Tokugawa Shoguns truly did fear that their power might be challenged by one of the great lords within their domain. Actually, that didn't happen for over two-and-a-half centuries. In **Ninja Scroll,** however, it happens much sooner. The contender is an evil magician who has the power to bring himself back from the dead and who hopes to rule Japan as the next Dark Shogun in a reign that would literally mean Hell on Earth. He is assisted in his aims by his "demons," *ninja* with startling supernatural abilities. Standing against him are a wily but elderly *ninja* from the Shogun's office, a beautiful female *ninja* named Kagerō whose touch means death, and quiet loner named Jūbei, a masterless *ninja* with merely human powers.

Ninja Scroll may have little relation to the actual history of the Tokugawa age it claims to depict, but it does introduce three heroic types drawn from the commoner tradition that emerge in many other *anime*. One, of course, is the wise, but not necessarily virtuous old man whom everyone underestimates. He can be found in many *anime* comedies from Happosai in **Ranma ¹/₂** to Grandpa Denbai in **Cutey Honey.** Kagerō 's poisoned touch is pretty unique, but her role as a tough female fighter out to avenge the deaths of those she loved, appears fairly often in characters like Priss of **Bubblegum Crisis/ Bubblegum Crash** or Ginrei in **Giant Robo.** As for Jūbei, he takes the samurai ideal and produces a populist version, a version in which simple decency wins out over money and rank. He is also a loner, a solitary warrior against the corruption of society at large. He has his followers in such characters as Ido in **Battle Angel,** or Captain Harlock in **Arcadia of My Youth.**

Black-clad *ninja* often appear in contemporary or futuristic *anime*, but rarely as individuals and almost never as heroes. Rumiko Takahashi finds *ninja* irresistibly funny. Mendou, the rich, handsome brat of her **Urusei Yatsura** series, is served by hordes of masked, faceless, black clad men who seem to be a cross between Kabuki stage hands (*kuroko*) and *ninja*. They are mindlessly obedient and carry out his every request in a literal-minded fashion. In one case, this results in thousands of take-out beef bowls, each individually wrapped and carried, being delivered to the high school. Kuno, the wealthy bully of **Ranma** $^1/_2$, also employs a *ninja*, Sasuke, as his trainer and henchman. Sasuke can do himself more damage falling from a tree than anyone else can do to him deliberately. When a female *ninja* appears in an episode of **Urusei Yatsura,** she is considerably cuter than Sasuke but no brighter. First she loses a secret scroll and then fails when she tries to use her female wiles on Ataru in an effort to get it back. Eventually she has to resort to a little known *ninja* technique involving stampeding pigs which ruins the scroll in the process of reclaiming it. *Ninja*, in Takahashi's view, clearly have no place in the modern world.

Osamu Yamazaki, the creator of **Akai Hayate** agrees with her, but his modern day *ninja* are no joke. They are a criminal underground, closely and corruptly connected with the Japanese government. Bound together in a group known as the Shinogara, they can buy and sell Prime Ministers. But all is not well with the Shinogara. Its leader is dead, murdered by his own son, Hayate, who is, in turn, killed by vengeful *ninja*. Factional fights turn ugly and threaten, in particular, a girl named Shiori, daughter of the slain leader, who carries within her her dead brother's spirit. True to the *ninja* tradition, the top Shinogara *ninja* have supernatural powers which vary from one member to the other. However, when they use these powers to battle it out in modern Tokyo instead of ancient Japan, the fact that they are thieves and murders rather than populist heroes tends to become obvious.

Fortunately, the warlord era also left another heroic, populist model, the peasant warriors who defended their own villages against bandits or marauding samurai. One of these is celebrated by Rumiko Takahashi in **Fire Tripper,** a Rumik World story about a modern schoolgirl who, after a gas explosion, finds herself not only living but loving in the past. Shukumaru, the peasant boy she comes to love, is a real roughneck, virtually illiterate and dressed in armor he stole from a corpse. Beneath the bluster, however, lies a gentle person with a greater sense of decency and honor than any samurai. You can almost hear Ranma coming around the corner. Shukumaru's futuristic heirs are found in such characters as Ran of **Green Legend Ran** and Hiro Seno of **The Venus Wars,** hot-headed young roughnecks with hearts of gold who leap to the defense of their homes and families.

Shukumaru, however, is of normal size and better than average good looks. An even more traditional form of this kind of peasant hero is revealed in Haohmaru of **Samurai Showdown.** He is a friendly giant, bulging with muscles, gentle to children, but able to strangle a bear with his hands if necessary. Like Shukumaru, he is uncouth in his manners, so much so that his resurrected comrades almost fail to recognize him as the reincarnation of the samurai who fought at Shimabara. Like Jūbei and Shukumaru, however, he has a simple decency and sense of honor that shames those who judge him by his outward appearance. Such simple giants have less validity in *anime* about contemporary or future societies, but they still turn up in characters like Tetsugyu in **Giant Robo** or even Briareos in **Appleseed.**

Other commoner heroes from Japan's feudal past are the *dōshin* assistants, the constables who patrolled urban streets during the Tokugawa era. The *dōshin* were the very lowest class of samurai. They patrolled the streets at night accompanied by their assistants, commoners hired and trained to do the dirty work, like fighting or actually arresting someone. Both the *dōshin* and their assistants carried a distinctive weapon, the *jitte*, a steel wand with a hook which they used to jerk swords from the hands of rowdy or drunken samurai. The *jitte* was also their badge which identified them as police.

No *anime* about historical *dōshin* assistants have yet made it to the American market. However, a futuristic offshoot has arrived in the form of **CyberCity Oedo 808** and the character of Benten. The action takes place in a future city called Oedo, or Greater Edo. Edo was the original name for Tokyo during the Tokugawa era. It was renamed Tokyo, which literally means "Eastern Capital," in 1868 when the Emperor took up residence there. Oedo is another way of saying "Neo-Tokyo." The

81

name, Benten, also has Tokugawa overtones. It does not, in this case, refer to the Taoist-Shinto goddess of the sea, but to "Benten Kozo" or "Benten the Thief," a popular Kabuki play from that era. The original Benten was not the androgynous gender-bender he becomes in **CyberCity Oedo,** but his most famous scene did involve dressing as a woman in order to make an escape. At the climax of the play, he throws off his woman's robes in a last defiant gesture.

In **CyberCity Oedo,** Benten keeps his female clothing on in a last defiant gesture. But his long, white hair hints back to the play. It could be a futuristic style, but it looks remarkably like a Kabuki wig. And, just in case anyone has still missed all the references to Tokugawa Japan, Benten carries a *jitte*. His appears to be sharpened and he uses it as sword. Indeed, in "The Vampire Case" episode, he poisons the tip of his *jitte* with a compound designed to break down the DNA of his mutant opponent. This is really more of a *ninja* trick, but it works.

Not all of Japan's warrior heroes or their villainous counterparts come from Japan's own past. Japan is a borrower culture and dubbed or subtitled foreign movies are high on the list of things most often borrowed. European films do tolerably well in Japan, but the two major countries of choice for imported films are Hong Kong and the United States. Between them, Chinese and American movies have provided *anime* with two new types of hero: the martial artist and the G.I.

Martial arts movies flood into Japan from both Hong Kong and the United States. By far the most popular, however, are the movies made by Jackie Chan in Hong Kong. A Chinese opera acrobat turned movie star and director, Chan has created a unique style of fast-paced, action-packed drama with a sense of humor that is only just beginning to be discovered in America. Chan, however, has been doing this sort of thing for close to twenty years and Japan has always provided his largest audience. Chan's more recent work tends toward crime dramas set in contemporary Hong Kong. His earlier movies, however, were usually historical in nature. They generally concerned a young man of low birth (played by Chan) who got beaten up by nearly everyone including the family cat. Eventually, the young man meets an elderly martial arts master down on his luck, and the two of them embark on a training program which often consisted of ridiculous and somewhat sadistic exercises that were pure slapstick.

Rumiko Takahashi obviously had some of these early Jackie Chan movies in mind when she created **Ranma ¹/₂**. Such martial arts training techniques as wrapping the novice in fish sausage and dropping him into a pit of hungry cats (cat-fu), or having him go jogging with a ball and chain attached to one leg are pure Chan. Indeed, although Ranma is identified by his last name as Japanese, he wears old-fashioned Chinese clothing, a pigtail, and even looks a lot like a young Jackie Chan, at least when he's in his male form. None of Chan's early characters ever changed sex although they did resort to dressing in drag from time to time. Shampoo, too, has her antecedents in Jackie Chan movies. Female martial artists like her are not uncommon in Hong Kong martial arts films generally, and Chan in particular used a lot of fighting women in his early movies.

Jackie Chan's form of *kung-fu* entertainment has been slow to catch on in America, probably because it draws the wrong audience. Those who might enjoy his zany sense of humor wouldn't be caught dead at a martial arts movie, and those who do go, tend to take the subject seriously and are sometimes offended by his light-hearted approach. This is a largely male audience who prefer the hard-boiled, no-holds-barred action of stars like the late Bruce Lee, Jean Claude van Damme and Chuck Norris, or Rambo movies. They may also like martial arts action *anime* like **Fatal Fury, Street Fighter,** and **Fist of the North Star,** or war films like **Area 88** or **The Dog Soldier.**

There's a good reason for that. These *anime* are actually based on American models in which brawny, not-too-bright men know no fear and feel no pain, and busty, not-too-bright women love them for it. So it's not surprising to find that one of these films is what introduced many *otaku* to *anime*. It's an easy first step. These American-style films seem familiar to young Americans because they are. Actually, the *anime* versions are sometimes an improvement over the American films they are trying to imitate, since they provide some aspects of *anime* out of sheer force of habit. **Fist of the North Star**, for example, may be the first time some American viewers realize that imagined horror is more terrifying than events actually depicted on screen. **Fist of the North Star** features plenty of graphic violence, most of it in the form of exploding heads, but the character whose head bulges and strains at the restraints that stop it from exploding is the one who excites the greatest horror. Female characters also play a more dramatic role even in these action *anime*. They always wind up as victims who need to be rescued and/or avenged, but before that they are allowed to demonstrate a reasonable amount of courage and fighting skills. The male characters, too, are a bit more interesting and varied. Some talk. Some even read and think. Some, like **Fatal Fury**'s Andy Bogard, combine muscles with an almost *bishōnen*-like beauty. Some viewers find that those features are even more entertaining than the action scenes and move on from these rather shallow *anime* to something more substantial.

Then they enter the world of the Japanese hero, a world filled with strange customs and assumptions. Why do they stay? Perhaps because it provides a model of heroism more in line with the realities of their own lives. The Japanese hero finds fulfillment in the act of loyalty, rather than in finding a cause or leader who will be worthy of that loyalty. That can be reassuring to young Americans who, increasingly, find that although they may believe in many causes, they can seldom find leaders who live up to their expectations.

In *anime*, they find an appropriately nihilistic view of society combined with a message of hope and glory. Government officials are invariably corrupt in the world of *anime*. The government may be represented by a warlord, a shogun, a prime minister, or the cyborg ruler of another planet, but it's never worthy of much respect. The economic sector does no better. In *anime* feudal merchants are a greedy lot, and future mega-corporations are even worse. But that doesn't prevent the young from being heroic. They may choose to resist the powers that be, or they may serve them on their own terms. What really matters is that they do it wholeheartedly. Now that's something in which even a Gen-Xer in a one-room apartment with a dead-end job at The Gap can find some inspiration.

Chapter Five

Androids, Cyborgs, and Other Mecha

The first *mecha*[1] to get a green card was **Astro Boy.** Together with his robot sister and numerous other robotic friends and relatives, he taught Americans that machines had feelings too. Many Baby Boomers today still have trouble saying goodbye to worn out cars and other gadgets because of what **Astro Boy** did to their impressionable young minds. **Astro Boy** was a real robot. It wasn't just that his body was made of metal, or that he had super strength, or that he could fly. His mind was also artificial, and so was his heart.[2] That only made him more lovable. Like Japanese, most Americans in the 1960s wanted to believe that human beings could duplicate Mother Nature's work, and probably do it better.

[1]*Mecha,* drawn from the English word "mechanical," is used by the Japanese to describe all forms of futuristic machines in *anime.* The word has since been adopted by American *otaku* for the same purpose.

[2]Later in the series there were a few plot twists suggesting ***Astro Boy*** didn't quite have the full complement of human emotions and, indeed, wanted them. In general, however, ***Astro Boy*** certainly acted as if he had feelings. They got hurt a lot.

[3](1) a robot may not injure a human being, or through inaction, allow a human being to come to harm, (2) a robot must obey the orders given it by human beings except where such orders would conflict with the First Law, (3) a robot must protect its own existence as long as such protection does not conflict with the First or Second Law.

[4]The reason they are called "boomers," or "boomah" in Japanese, is obscure in ***Bubblegum Crisis.*** Apparently this puzzled the Japanese, too. When the Knight Sabers returned in a new series, ***Bubblegum***

continued

That dream died in America and it's begun to die in Japan, too. Few of the so-called robots seen in contemporary *anime* really are robots in the fullest sense. They are not, as a rule, machine bodies with machine minds. Robots who look and act more or less like human beings, robots like ***Astro Boy,*** are rare in *anime* these days. And when they do occur, their humanity is a far more complex matter than that of ***Astro Boy*** who simply loved and wanted to be loved. ***Armitage III,*** for example, is a fully artificial android, but she looks, acts, and feels like a young woman, a lethal young woman with a very itchy trigger finger. The same is true of other "thirds," advanced robots like her. They are more like improved human beings than machines: brilliant, sensitive, and often creative, but they have obviously never heard of Isaac Asimov's Three Laws of Robotics.[3] For the "thirds," their own survival comes first. And if that isn't human, what is?

This is less true of Antoinette, the mechanical heroine of ***The Humanoid.*** Antoinette is more obviously robotic. Although shaped like a woman, her complexion is unabashedly chromium. And her mind, too, seems to be a machine mind, logical and without feeling. That, however, turns out to be simply the result of youth. As Antoinette comes of age, she learns to feel emotions and also learns how to disobey. By the time she makes her ultimate sacrifice to save her planet, she is emotionally sappy enough to induce a diabetic coma.

Armitage and Antoinette are fairly isolated examples in the world of *anime,* however. Most robots who are completely artificial are also completely evil, or at least unreliable. The "boomers" of ***Bubblegum Crisis/Bubblegum Crash*** are typical.[4] Originally designed to help humanity, they have long since been monopolized by an evil corporation and turned to military purposes. And even at that, they don't work. They are forever going on the rampage, shooting up innocent civilians and destroying urban areas. They are the whole reason for the existence of the Knight Sabers and the A.D. Police. Pure *mecha* usually equals pure menace.

Most of the *mecha* seen in *anime* are actually some sort of armor, an external skeleton with enormous strength, but controlled by a human brain or sometimes a team of human brains. The efficacy of *mecha* is not necessarily linked to size.

The power suits worn by the Knight Sabers in **Bubblegum Crisis/Bubblegum Crash** are form-fitting, high-heeled suits of armor with a few wires here and there. Designed by Silia Stingray and based on her dead father's theories, those power suits are what give the Knight Sabers the strength to fight the Boomers when they run amok. Oh, they train and work to stay in shape (except maybe Nene who can't even stay on a diet), but their real strength derives from the way these power suits increase the speed and strength of any blow they strike.

Crash, an introductory voice-over explained that they were so named because their creation originally resulted in an economic boom for humanity.

Most *anime* power suits are larger than those used by the Knight Sabers. The typical *anime* power suit looks more like a robot. The only difference is that it contains a command chair, usually somewhere in the chest region. The pilot is hooked up to a variety of wires that cause the robot to duplicate and magnify any movement he or she makes.

Anime women have a particular affinity for this type of *mecha*, and no wonder. Power suits provide the upper body strength most women lack. Dressed in power suits, men and women become equals as warriors. Size and physical strength becomes irrelevant. Victory becomes a question of courage, intelligence, and skill.

Power suits also allow female warriors to retain their femininity without being rendered passive. Power suits allow the all-female Solenoids of the first three episodes of **Gall Force** to perform prodigious feats of strength and derring-do with never a muscle to mar the perfection of their slim bodies. The pirate women of the **Sol Bianca** find a more prosaic use for their power suits. They use them for loading and unloading as well as fighting. It saves strain and allows them to keep their stylish outfits neat and clean.

Such power suits are really exoskeletons. Those used by the Knight Sabers do not even increase the size of the women much. They are simply a rather bulky item of clothing. The power suits used by the Solenoids and the crew of the **Sol Bianca** are more obviously robotic. They are at least three or four times the size of the women who use them and include a pilot's seat. Such suits can get much bigger. They can become gigantic, space-going robots.

Probably the best known example of this form of *mecha* doesn't come from *anime* at all. It's the Megazord from the **Mighty Morphin Power Rangers**, itself a transplant from Japanese TV. Formed from the combined avatars of the five power rangers, the Megazord is a huge fighting machine in the shape of an armored samurai. The power rangers direct its movements from a control room located in its chest. The Megazord itself shows little sign of having any intelligence of its own, beyond an ability to come when called. It is totally mechanical. It is pure *mecha*.

The Megazord comes from an illustrious line of Japanese *mecha*. Its ancestors include **Gigantor,** the **Macross** (**Robotech**) flying fortress, and **Gundam**.[5] And *anime* continues to produce series centered on Megazord-style robots. **Gunbuster,** for example, begins at the Space High School for Girls, where young women are trained to operate huge space-going robots which exaggerate each movement they make a hundredfold. The heroine, Noriko Takaya, is a slow learner, but she perseveres and is eventually assigned to the **Gunbuster,** an experimental model which requires two pilots. Noriko's partner is a beautiful and talented young woman, Kazumi Amano. Thereafter, **Gunbuster** focuses primarily on the relationship between the two women as they struggle to balance their personal and professional lives. The **Gunbuster** itself has no real personality, although Noriko does apologize to it as she and Kazumi prepare for a final *kamikaze* attack which may or may not kill them, but which will certainly destroy their ship.

[5]**Gundam,** a long running series loosely centered around a type of robot-shaped spaceship of that name, has never been officially released in the United States. However, fan-subs are so prolific that even *otaku* who don't speak Japanese are familiar with it.

The same is true in **Patlabor**. The huge construction robots called "labors" have no wills of their own. They are vehicles, driven and manipulated by human beings. So when they go out of control in the first **Patlabor** movie, the **Patlabor** police look for a human culprit and they find one. To disable the rampaging labors, they have to use other robots, robots that may or may not have been infected with the virus that's causing the problem in the first place. That can be nerve wracking, but there's no sense that the robots themselves are to blame. They aren't people. They're just *mecha*.

Other crews have a somewhat more personal relationship with their *mecha*. Roll Kran, Miya Alice, Rambo Nom, and Pi Thunder, the four psychics who pilot the **Dangaio** robot certainly do. Of course, their contributions are more personal. In order to even form the **Dangaio** robot, they must synchronize their minds and hearts. **Dangaio** is nothing less than the sum of their fused selves. The robot is the means by which they are able to merge their humanity and turn it to a useful purpose, but there is a price. Pi Thunder must give up her treasured independence to create **Dangaio**; later, she also renounces her father. Mia Alice gives up her chance to return to her old home on Earth. Roll

Kran, the group's only male member, undergoes a remarkable transformation from wimp to macho man. That may be seen as an improvement, and it's certainly necessary since he sits in the command chair, but he isn't very happy about it and it affects his relationship with the others. For the *Dangaio* team, their contribution to assembling and operating the robot is intensely personal. That necessarily affects their feelings for the robot. However, the robot itself remains pure *mecha*. The feelings the crew express toward it reflect their feelings for one another.

Dangaio and the labors are fairly sophisticated robots in both technology and appearance. More recently, there has been a preference among *mecha* fans for more nuts, bolts, and gears. *Anime* such as *Giant Robo* and *Kishin Corps* deliberately create *mecha* that are more clearly and obviously mechanical. This makes perfect sense in *Kishin Corps* where World War II in China is interrupted by the landing of hostile aliens in Manchuria. Japan allies with Great Britain and the United States to combat the menace using a variety of robots. The plot doesn't make much sense and the historical interpretation doesn't bear discussing, but the *mecha* are fantastic. True to the era, the *Kishin Corps* robots are Art Deco masterpieces of intermeshing gears, bolted connections, and manual controls. Except for Fu, the single-pilot flying robot, they all require a skilled crew to operate them. The other *mecha*, trains, planes, ships, cars, and the like, all share the same retro-*mecha* styling. It fits. The story, after all, plays in the early 1940s, even if it's not quite the same 1940s the history books have recorded.

That's not true of *Giant Robo* which plays in the future. Admittedly, it is the near future, but one that has been greatly changed by the invention of the Shizuma drive, a completely efficient, nonpolluting form of energy. It sounds perfect, but it isn't. When a criminal organization devises a means of stopping all Shizuma drives, they hold the entire world hostage. Everything runs on Shizuma energy, everything except *Giant Robo* who, it transpires, is still powered by nuclear energy. He was deliberately made old-fashioned in order to deal with precisely this kind of emergency. In keeping with that purpose, *Giant Robo*'s appearance is also retro-*mecha*. He is a huge creature of red and grey metal held together with nuts and bolts. His operator, a boy named Daisuke, rides on his shoulder hanging on to the metal rungs that run up the side of his head. *Giant Robo* doesn't even have an interior cockpit. Daisuke communicates with *Giant Robo* using a wrist-watch radio . . . with an antenna, no less!

The other *mecha* in **Giant Robo** are equally retro. The laser beams with which the heroes try to stop the Shizuma drive destroyer are huge blown-glass light bulbs with ornate, colored designs. The creator of **Giant Robo** claims to have been inspired by **The Rocky Horror Picture Show**, but his *mecha* look more like Jules Verne inventions than anything else. The same is true of the background sets. In **Giant Robo**, postmodern architecture has gone wild. Buildings are huge, ornate structures of beveled glass and cupolas. Even the characters' costumes have a retro look. The men wear suits with nipped in waists, except when they go even further back to traditional Japanese or Chinese costumes. Ginrei, the only woman in **Giant Robo**, wears an ankle-length Chinese dress except in battle when she is more scantily clad. Everything, of course, requires manual control. That's the whole point of retro-*mecha*, to put people back in charge.

Of course, people don't always want to be in charge. Some *mecha* acquire their human pilots by simply refusing to take no for an answer. This is most often true with alien robots like Organ in **Detonator Organ**.[6] Organ is an Evoluder, a member of an alien race that has long since merged with machine bodies. This has not improved their dispositions. The Evoluder enjoy nothing more than destroying other people's planets, and Earth is next on their list. Fortunately, one of their number, a particularly powerful fighting machine named Organ, has turned traitor. He heads for Earth in order to fight against his own kind, but he doesn't quite make it. He is blown apart on Mars. In a last-ditch effort, he sends his own blueprints to Earth where they are decoded by an attractive young scientist, Professor Tanizaki. She not only decodes the blueprints, she builds the machine which, however, is incomplete without its biological component. It becomes whole only when it incorporates a human being, in this case a young man named Tomoru, into its structure. This is not a move that sits well with Tomoru. Organ, after all, was an Evoluder soldier before he turned traitor, and to share his blood-soaked, murderous memories is disturbing, to say the least. Tomoru sticks it out, largely because he has fallen in love with Professor Tanizaki, but he goes through numerous fits of adolescent angst along the way.

[6]In fact, the Japanese reads more like Oh-gahn. The distributors probably couldn't resist.

At least Tomoru has some say in the matter. Sho Fukamachi of **The Guyver** is never offered any sort of choice at all. He simply finds the *mecha* and accidentally triggers it. Thereafter, **The Guyver** becomes a part of his body. **The Guyver** is not really *mecha* in the fullest sense of the word. The title describes it as "bio-booster armor," and it certainly looks quite painfully biological as it wraps itself around and incorporates with Sho's body. *The Guyver* gives Sho tremendous strength and superpowers, but it turns him into a biologically engineered monstrosity. He can return to his normal schoolboy appearance, but he lives in dread that his girlfriend will find out what he has become. Fortunately for him, she eventually winds up with a guyver of her own, but the biological nature of *The Guyver* makes it far more grisly than anything made of metal.

That is even more true of *Genocyber*, a monstrosity created by a brutal experiment involving two sisters. The experimenter is their father, a man who put the "d" in dysfunctional family relations. As a result of an earlier experiment, neither of his daughters is quite normal. One is physically healthy, but has the mind of an animal, all instinct, no reason. She has run away and lives wild among the homeless in the slums of Hong Kong. Her sister is all mind. She has to be. Her body is pure *mecha*, an experimental mechanism with which her father tinkers, blithely ignoring her screams of pain. Both girls, as it transpires, have psionic powers and, for reasons that are never made clear, they hate each other as well as their father. Partly by accident and partly by design, they become merged into the creature known as *Genocyber*. Under normal circumstances they exist in the body of the healthy sister, mindless and occasionally happy. However, when danger threatens, they become *Genocyber* and the carnage begins.

Actually *Genocyber* has a rough but accurate sense of justice. She generally weighs in on the side of the oppressed, but she is overly prone to destroying the village (or city or country or planet) in order to save it.[7] *Genocyber* is more than an external suit, she is an alien entity created from human mind and flesh. She is an obscene monstrosity, rendered all the more monstrous because she is, at the same time, human and vulnerable.

Akira also deals with the dangers of genetic engineering. *Akira* is probably the best known and least well understood example of *anime* in America. It plays regularly on campuses, in art houses, and even in mainstream movie theaters. Many Americans who are otherwise unfamiliar with *anime* have seen *Akira*. However, the reasons *Akira* has received such prominent billing are its technical excellence and the fact that it has been more aggressively marketed than most *anime*.

Americans for whom *Akira* is their first exposure to *anime* usually also give it high marks for creativity in its plot line.

[7]*Genocyber* actually looks more male than female, and "it" would not be an unsuitable pronoun. However, since it is composed of two women, it's hard to see how it could be anything other than female.

Real *otaku* know better. They are not surprised by the ending which is unresolved, unfair, and never fully explained. That happens a lot in *anime*. Moreover, they recognize that ***Akira***'s plot is typical of a whole school of science fiction *anime* which warns of the dangers of combining human and artificial intelligence. It's a good example of what that school can do, but it's not atypical. The world of ***Akira*** is typical of many futuristic dystopias in *anime*. Nuclear war has devastated the planet and gangs rule the city streets. It seems as if things can't get any worse until Tetsuo, a young gang member, stumbles across an artificially created genetic mutation called ***Akira*** which releases the psionic potential in his mind. Then, things do get worse. Much worse. In many ways, Tetsuo's predicament is similar to that of ***Genocyber*** except that his alter-ego is an artificial entity rather than a human sister, however hated. Mixing human and artificial minds is seldom wise in *anime*, and ***Akira*** is no exception. The fact that other mutants, whose survival depends on the rebirth of the ***Akira*** pattern in Tetsuo's brain, use their telepathic powers to confuse him doesn't help. Tetsuo can't cope with the changes that are going on in his mind to start with. Eventually he explodes literally as well as figuratively, and takes the rest of his nightmarish world with him. We never really learn what the ***Akira*** pattern was supposed to accomplish for humanity.

The same is true of the psionic "head meters" in ***Ai City***. The movie never really clarifies how they have been altered, but the presence of digital readouts on their foreheads certainly suggests some mixing of human and mechanical elements. That's even more obviously true of the two lead villains. One simply sports a larger than average array of cyborg augmentations that enclose his head in a painful looking metal mask. The other, however, has become a tiny naked man in a bowl of pink jello atop a robotic body. As is the case in ***Akira***, this mixing of humanity with *mecha* bodes ill for the future. Only the intervention of a little girl who holds the unknown power of "***Ai City***" in her DNA, her "father" who has never had a child, a dirty old man, a woman in a Playboy bunny suit, and a cat wearing a leather jacket and sunglasses can save Earth from a fate worse than ***Akira***. At least, they seem to. ***Ai City***'s ending makes ***Akira***'s ending look crystal clear.

Hades Project Zeorymer combines the fear of genetically engineered life forms with the fear of more traditional *mecha*. It features a dystopic future in which there is little to choose between a despotic, murderous government and a despotic, murderous underworld. Masato Akitsu grew up in that world, but he's not really ready for it. Who would be? At age sixteen, he must come to grips with the fact that he was grown in a test-tube, genetically coded to pilot the Zeorymer, a powerful fighting robot stolen from a criminal organization by the government. Masato is a gentle soul, but the government officials force him into the pilot's seat. Zeorymer, although essentially mindless in itself, immediately downloads its only program, the memory and personality of its megalomaniacal creator, into the unfortunate boy. Thereafter, Masato must fight not only the underworld robots and the Japanese government, but an alien personality that is overwhelming him from within. Eventually, Masato's humanity triumphs over this grim legacy when he joins his equally tormented clone-sister in suicide.

Masato was the victim of two forms of human tampering, first through his artificial birth and second, through his union with a machine. Union with a machine can be enough. Mr. Takazawa, the elderly hero of **Roujin Z**, is a normal human being. He's just old, confused, and ready to die. Too bad someone hooked him into a robotic life support system with connections to military hardware. Programmed to respond to the old man's every wish, the life support unit does its best to see that he gets what he wants and needs. It's a pity that he only wants to rejoin his dead wife for a day at the beach. Neither the old man's point of view nor the robot's is unreasonable. However, when they are joined into a cyborg that takes on the persona of Mr. Takazawa's dead wife, carnage ensues.

Most Americans understand the fear that artificial intelligence and genetic engineering will get out of control. Many share it. They may have a harder time understanding the Japanese attitude toward organ transplants and artificial replacements which forms a major theme in many science fiction *anime*. In Japan, organ transplants are a highly emotional issue, rather like the abortion debate in America. It's not as politicized, but most Japanese have strong feelings on the subject that predate whatever rational arguments they may make. That's not to say there is no rational side to the argument. Opponents argue that organ transplants can, and indeed, already have, led to abuses. Americans have little trouble understanding that argument. Most probably agree with it. However, Americans see the development of artificial organs as a solution. As can be seen in *anime* like **Akira**, **Ai City**, and **Roujin Z**, that possibility makes many Japanese even more nervous. Their objection to organ transplants is not entirely rational. It is also based on a deep, visceral repulsion born of Confucian beliefs regarding the need to go whole to one's grave and Shinto ideas about physical purity.

That revulsion takes physical form in *anime* depictions of cyborgs.

Leiji Matsumoto addressed the issue directly and explicitly in *Galaxy Express 999,* a science fiction story about a future in which many humans have transferred their minds to android bodies and thus achieved immortality.[8] In doing so, however, they have sacrificed their humanity. One of the most affecting characters in *Galaxy Express 999* is Shadow, a ghostly, faceless cyborg woman who haunts the icy graveyards of Pluto vainly searching for her cast-off human body. She accosts humans who visit there, desperately clutching them, trying to absorb some small part of their warmth.

The nightmarish world of *Battle Angel* reveals an even stronger repugnance with its graphic depictions of stored organs and spines being ripped from still living bodies. It's hard to say which is the more monstrous, the wealthy elites who buy such parts without asking where they come from, or the desperate slum dwellers who prey on each other to provide them. The slum dwellers themselves make do with artificial parts. That doesn't always help. Some of the most ghastly monsters are the enhanced cyborgs who fight in the arena. Other cyborgs are treated more kindly. When a street urchin named Yugo is severely injured and has most of his body replaced, he is portrayed sympathetically as a victim who has undergone a difficult and painful, but necessary, medical procedure. The heroine, Gally, falls somewhere in between. She is a total cyborg, an altered, programmed human brain in a completely artificial body. Whether this was a medical procedure or something done to her to make her a more effective warrior is not clear. Gally herself doesn't know. She has no memory. She is an appealing, sympathetic character, an innocent trying to make the best life she can for herself in a world she never made. Yukito Kishiro, the creator of *Battle Angel*, clearly finds the idea of combining human beings with artificial parts repulsive, but his repulsion does not necessarily extend to those who have had it done.

A.D. Police, the prequel to *Bubblegum Crisis/Bubblegum Crash* also reveals mixed feelings about organ replacement.[9] The second episode of *A.D. Police,* "The Ripper," consists of two interrelated plots. One concerns the decision facing Ailis Kara, a policewoman

[8] A dubbed version of *Galaxy Express 999* was released under the title *Galaxy Express* as a children's classic in 1979 by New World Pictures. It is no longer in print but can sometimes be found in rental outlets. It was heavily edited to hide its Japanese origins and many *otaku* consider it too damaged to watch. The animation remains spectacular, however, and Matsumoto's dark, heart-wrenching themes of death and impermanence, loss and loneliness, and the ambiguity of good and evil still comes through well enough to move adults and make it a questionable choice for children. Actually, some parents praise *Galaxy Express* for raising these issues in a way children can understand, but agree that the first showing should be supervised and followed by discussion.

who needs, but fears, an artificial eye implant. While she debates that matter, she searches for someone who has been murdering and mutilating prostitutes. One of her suspects is a female executive who has had herself reconstructed from the waist down in order to assuage fears that her periods and/or pregnancies might make her unreliable. This ruthless act resulted in a meteoric career, but now the woman has married and begun to regret her decision. Indeed, she fears that her hardware is now controlling her, possibly forcing her to commit the murders. Is she mad, or is she right? As Ailis learns more about her suspect and the full ramifications of artificial body parts, she makes a surprising decision about her own surgery.

A.D. Police also includes a chilling tale of a policeman who has been so rebuilt that the only human sensation he can still experience is when he bites his tongue. Robot-hating Ross Sylibus of **Armitage III** also worries about the increasing number of artificial parts he seems to be acquiring. In general, however, men take cyborg adaptations more coolly than women. For women, the problem is usually sexual. They wonder about their appearance, their fertility, and the effect their great strength has on the men they care about.

This is certainly the case with Kiddy Phenil, the strong woman of the A.M.P.[10] police force in **Silent Möbius**.[11] Her body is almost completely artificial, something she hides from a young man who is fascinated by her strength and determined to find out the reason for it. Eventually, Kiddy decides to face him with the truth. She uses a blowtorch to melt the synthetic flesh from the metal. The young man is appalled at first, but he makes the adjustment. Even more surprisingly, so does Kiddy.

Americans and Japanese share many of the same concerns about runaway technology, artificial intelligence, robots, genetic engineering, and cyborg parts. Both have nightmares as well as dreams about the future applications of such technologies, and both bring those nightmares and dreams to the screen. Americans often ignore that similarity. Japan has been idolized as a nation at peace with the future, a "robot kingdom" without the doubts that plague Americans. *Anime* makes it clear that this is untrue. Because of different assumptions and cultural mores, the Japanese sometimes have somewhat different fears about the future, but they have just as many.

[9]*A.D. Police* is set before the events recounted in **Bubblegum Crisis/Bubble gum Crash,** but it was actually produced after that series was complete.

[10]A.M.P. stands for Attack Mystification Police, a futuristic corps of mediums, exorcists, and other demon busters.

[11]This episode of **Silent Möbius** is not yet out in animated form. The *manga* version is available from Viz Communication.

Chapter Six

Death and Other Bad Stuff

A funny thing happened in the first episode of **Star Blazers**. Two fine, heroic people died. Yes, died! Now, that was something you didn't see every day on 1980s television. Oh, there was a lot of violence and people got killed on a regular basis, but you didn't really watch them die. You didn't have to deal with the consequences of death.

Those who died on American TV were generally unpleasant people, and/or relative strangers to both the audience and the main characters. **Star Trek** fans called them "phaser bait," unfamiliar characters introduced for one episode only so that they could die or have something else unpleasant happen to them. No one knew much about who they'd been or what they'd wanted except for the immediate

97

circumstances (usually careless or reprehensible) that brought about their deaths. That way no one had to dwell on the things they had left uncompleted or the tragedy of a life cut prematurely short. No one had to go through the whole complex business of mourning.

Except on **Star Blazers**. Dead or not, Alex Wildstar lived on in his younger brother's memory.[1] We learned what kind of person he had been and why he had been loved. We saw what his death did to his brother. We saw that people in mourning, even heroes in mourning, don't necessarily behave well. Derek Wildstar didn't. He blamed the wrong person for his brother's death, striking out blindly and cruelly at Captain Avatar, oblivious to the fact that the captain was already devastated by Alex's fate.

And the situation got worse. A flashback showed how Derek's parents had died. They were struck by a bomb while waiting at the bus stop for their son to come home. One moment they were there, the next they were gone, stupidly, pointlessly gone. We waited for them to crawl out of the wreckage but they didn't. And then it transpired that the captain was terminally ill with radiation poisoning. He chose to forgo the medical treatment that might have saved him in order to lead the expedition to Iskandar. The others at least stood a chance of survival, but the captain knew when they left that he would never see Earth or his family again. No one believed it at first. Conditioned by American TV codes, young Americans confidently waited for a reprieve. Dr. Sane would develop a cure or one would be discovered en route. But that didn't happen. The captain was expected to die and he did.[2] Fans loved it.

[1] Okay, Alex Wildstar wasn't really dead but no one knew that until the end of the series.

[2] Captain Avatar was resurrected in **Final Yamato**, a movie made eleven years after the episode in which he died. His resurrection was an unexpected result of the *Yamato* series' unprecedented longevity. In any case, **Final Yamato** was never part of the **Star Blazers** series as it aired on American TV.

And *otaku* continue to love that aspect of *anime*, the fact that bad things, even death, can happen to any character at any time. It doesn't matter how brave, how good, or even how popular they are. And the deaths aren't always as heroic as Captain Avatar's which at least fits into the samurai tradition of self-sacrifice. Many *anime* characters meet meaningless, shabby, undeserved ends.

That doesn't happen on American television where virtue is inevitably rewarded and evil punished. That's partly because of TV codes and actors' contracts. But it's also because America is a Judeo-Christian culture which believes that the universe is, or at least should be, a moral place. The reason politicians and the television industry won't let bad guys get away with it or good guys die is that it might lead viewers, especially children, to believe that the universe doesn't care. And that, in turn, would undermine the nation's morality because it suggests that God is indifferent, irrational, or not the only creator around. After all, if God made both human beings and the universe, both should operate according to the same morality. If you suggest that the universe is amoral, you also imply that it's all right for people to be the same way.

The Japanese don't worry about that. Their view is that the universe is amoral and the sooner we all accept it, the better. *Anime* reflects the Japanese view of morality as clearly as American television codes reflect Judeo-Christian concerns. As with the American view of the moral universe, the Japanese amoral one is based in the nation's religious and philosophical traditions. Shinto has no moral code at all; it simply celebrates life. Buddhism does have a moral code, but the way it's practiced in Japan downplays that side of things.

That sometimes leads Americans to assume that the Japanese themselves are amoral or possibly immoral. It means nothing of the sort. It simply means that they don't carry their moral code in their religion. Instead, their ideas of right and wrong are based on human social relationships, an idea loosely adapted from Chinese Confucianism. To the Japanese, morality is a purely human concept, a social concept. It's not tied to any transcendental view of the universe. People and the universe are two different things and play by different rules. Heroism and self-sacrifice define an *anime* character as a hero, but they will not save him or her. The universe simply doesn't care.

That's why Captain Avatar died. His willingness to sacrifice his life to save the Earth was heroic and virtuous in human terms, and those who knew of it honored him for it. The universe, however, simply took note of the fact that his body had absorbed more radiation than was consistent with survival, and ran right over him.

That happens a lot in *anime*. American heroes can feel secure in offering to embark on seemingly suicidal missions. Their moral universe will probably save them from having to make the ultimate sacrifice. And even if it doesn't, it will certainly ensure that the sacrifice will not have been in vain. When *anime* heroes offer up their lives, they had better mean it. They will almost certainly die, and there is no guarantee that their sacrifice will actually achieve what they hope it will.

Nor is gender any protection in *anime*. The universe doesn't care about that either. Even when it's a lovely, innocent schoolgirl like Miki in **Ambassador Magma**, the universe still doesn't care. Miki carries the right genetic code to resurrect the giant golden robot that is Earth's last chance for survival. Her death is necessary. The fact that she accepts this and goes to it willingly is what defines her as a hero. But it does not save her, and there is no guarantee that the giant robot actually can or will save the Earth.

Miki's death does not go unmourned. She has a sweetheart, Mamoru Asuka, who rails helplessly against the injustice of it all. Actually, Mamoru does get some response from the universe. Father Earth appears to him and tries to console him with the revelation that Miki has now become a star in the Heavens. Unfortunately, what the universe considers as consolation is not what humans find consoling. Mamoru is an adolescent just awakening to the possibilities of love, and stars are of no use to him whatsoever. His mourning reflects everything Miki might have been and now will never be. And there is little consolation in that.

Both Miki and Captain Avatar go to their deaths knowingly and for altruistic reasons. Their deaths are incontestably heroic. The universe isn't always that kind, not even to people who are heroes in other ways. Indeed, some *anime* suggest that sudden, youthful death is far from being the worst of fates.

GoShogun: The Time Étranger, for example, reintroduces a hero from an early giant robot series, Remy Shimada. Once a proud member of the GoShogun team, she and her comrades saved the Earth more than once with their giant robot.[3] And they survived. Now, forty years later, that survival is revealed to be a mixed blessing. Remy in particular has taken retirement hard. At age seventy, she tries to recreate the excitement of her youth by risky behavior such as reckless driving and ignoring her health. Finally, while racing to a belated reunion with her old comrades, she crashes her car and finds herself in a sinister city which, it transpires, is the last stop before death.

In fact, the city is in her mind. She herself lies dying in a hospital bed. Her former comrades regroup to pressure an indifferent medical system to give her a fighting chance at life. In so doing, they reveal a lot of the corruption and compromises that have marked their own development since their heroic GoShogun days. The contrast is all the more marked since they also appear as their more idealistic, youthful selves in Remy's mind.[4] For them, survival has meant an end to heroism. Only Remy, it transpires, has resisted the lure of fame and wealth. Only Remy held on to her principles until the end.

[3] A dubbed version of earlier GoShogun adventures is available under the title **Macron I.**

[4] None of the characters in **GoShogun: The Time Étranger** look as old as the script claims them to be. Nonetheless, their "real life" selves have a used, tired look, while their younger "dream" selves still glow with idealism.

And now Remy is dying an ignominious death in a hospital bed tended by uncaring strangers.

GoShogun: The Time Étranger is probably the clearest example of the Japanese view of death, justice, and the universe. In the course of Remy Shimada's struggle to escape the death city, she recalls other incidents in which she narrowly escaped death. These, in turn, reveal the life that made her the kind of person she is. Although it is about death, **GoShogun: The Time Étranger** is a celebration of life. It is the immediacy of death that makes life doubly precious. That won't necessarily save Remy. She has less than a 1 percent chance of making it. And, as the universe speaking through the persona of the death city police chief regularly reminds her, even if she does triumph this time, she will be back. She is mortal and this is one fight she will inevitably lose.

Remy is not alone. Many *anime* characters meet less than heroic deaths and the best they can do about it is to die with dignity. In **Battle Angel**, a street urchin named Yugo is given only seconds in which to understand the value of life and love before plunging to his death upon a metal scrap heap. Yugo is not an entirely admirable character. He has spent his life trying to amass enough money to live in the floating pleasure city above the scrap heap slums in which he was born. To achieve that goal, he has stolen, killed, and ignored everything else of value including the selfless love of Gally, the "battle angel" of the title.[5] After a series of disasters which destroy his body and leave him more machine than human being, he makes one last, desperate attempt to reach the city of his dreams by climbing the huge transport tube that connects it to the ground. His attempt is foiled by the tube's anti-vermin device, sharp rotating rings that destroy his rebuilt android legs. Gally races to his side, but the two have only seconds together. Gally suggests that even life in a slum like the scrap heap below can be paradise if there is love. At long last, Yugo realizes she is right and reaches out to her. At that moment, a second anti-vermin device descends. Gally is still agile enough to avoid it, but Yugo, already seriously wounded, is torn to shreds. Gally risks her own life to save him, but he refuses to put her in further danger. "I am happy to have known you," he tells her, "good-bye." Then the last cord in his artificial arm snaps and he plunges soundlessly to his death.

[5]Gally was renamed "Alita" in the translated *manga.*

For some *anime* characters, death is a choice. The Japanese attitude toward suicide is markedly different from that of Americans. To those raised in a Judeo-Christian tradition, suicide is a sin, a rejection of God's greatest gift. At best, it can be chalked up to insanity. More frequently, it is seen as cowardice.

The typical Japanese view of suicide is very different. For the samurai, ritual suicide was an honorable choice, a way to redeem lost honor. The same is true of suicide missions in battle situations. Actually, that is the one area in which Americans might agree, although even American war movies rarely show a character deliberately choosing death. More frequently, American war heroes are simply placed in a situation where saving their own life would cost someone else theirs. *Anime* is not so squeamish. When human civilization is threatened in **Giant Robo**, for example, Taisō makes a clear choice to stay in order to keep a defective machine on target, rather than escape with his comrades. There is no question that he will die. He says goodbye to his wife, Yoshi, who honors his decision and does not mourn. There's a good reason for that. She has no intention of surviving him for long. She remains alive only long enough to make her death count. As it turns out, however, both Taisō and Yoshi's deaths are in vain. Their efforts fail to stop the orb that threatens humanity's survival. But that doesn't make their deaths any less courageous or honorable.

That doesn't mean all suicides are honorable. Those who commit suicide over lost loves or failed college exams are not seen as heroic. Such suicides, although still not regarded as sinful, are regarded as pathetic. Depending on the circumstances, they may also be seen as selfish.

Some deaths fall midway between the pathetic and fully honorable. In **Toward the Terra**, for example, Keith is a man bred and programmed by the mad Mother-Computer Eliza to defend the status quo. When he at last recognizes that fact and decides to die in defiance of his programming, he makes the only really independent decision of his life. His death serves no actual purpose. It neither restores his honor nor does anyone any good. It is a personal statement, a last attempt to give meaning to a life that otherwise had none. The same is true of Yuratei and Masato in **Hades Project Zeorymer**. Both have been artificially cloned by and from a mad genius. Both have been genetically programmed to live lives at odds with their true desires. Their continued existence also threatens humanity's survival, but essentially Yuratei forces a showdown with Masato because dying is the only way she can avoid the destiny built into her DNA. Masato answers her challenge and dies with her for the same reason. For people like Keith, Yuratei, and Masato, choosing death is choosing freedom. In *anime*, a premature death is often the only way in which a mere human can defeat fate.

The same is true in a different way for Prince Roland and Princess Veronica in **Windaria**. They love each other desperately, but each is bound by a deathbed oath to wage war against the other. In the end, Princess Veronica understands that death is the only answer. She kills her lover and then herself. Any Kabuki fan would recognize her predicament. She is in a classic conflict between duty (*giri*) and human feelings (*ninjō*). This is the same conflict that actually led to a number of double suicides in feudal Japan. For lovers in a *giri-ninjō* bind, death not only provided an answer, but also registered a protest against the social constraints that put them in such an impossible situation. Then, Kabuki carried that protest to the public. Today, *anime* provides the same service.

Actually, **Windaria**'s view of death is unusual in that it promises some sort of desirable afterlife to those who die. Most *anime* don't. Pure Land Buddhism, the most popular form of Buddhism practiced in Japan, has a clearly articulated vision of Heaven and Hell. Shinto, however, sees Yomi, the land of the dead, as a dark place, a place of decay and corruption, a place of no return. The clearest view of the Shinto underworld is presented in Japan's original creation myth. When the goddess Izanami died, her husband/brother was so grief-stricken that he followed her into the underworld to try to get her back. She greeted him in the darkness and assured him of her love, but warned him not to strike a light in order to look at her. He immediately did just that and saw that the woman he had loved had become a rotting corpse. He fled in horror pursued by her angry curses. The Japanese story is similar in many ways to the Greek myth of Orpheus in the underworld except that the Japanese version offers no suggestion that Izanami might ever have returned to the land of the living. There is no evidence to suggest any connection. Both stories simply reflect the natural horror people feel toward what death does to a body that was once loved and desirable.

In *anime*, the Shinto view predominates. Death is the end and even the most heroic characters do not try to follow their loved ones past the grave. The dead can offer little in the way of comfort to the living. If they are lucky, they may have a chance to say good-bye. This is certainly the case with Katsumi Liqueur in **Silent Möbius**. Katsumi's spiritual powers allow her to enter the astral plane for a final word with her dying mother. Her mother struggles to make the moment a positive one. She assures her daughter of her love and urges her to be strong, but she says nothing about a further meeting. At the end, she says the only thing the dead can say, the same thing Yugo said to Gally: "Good-bye."

Even when the Buddhist afterlife is depicted, it is more likely to be the Buddhist version of Hell than Heaven. Indeed, this has historically been the case. Although some *mandala* depict a stylized view of paradise, Hell gets much more coverage. Most ancient temples feature at least one good example of a medieval "hell-scroll," a painting in which the sufferings of the damned are depicted in meticulous detail.[6] As with European medieval art, the demons provided better subject matter than the saints.

[6]The tradition of hell-scroll painting has had a revival recently in the work of Toshi and Iri Maruki who paint one each year as part of their anti-nuclear campaign. The Marukis, however, do not paint an imaginary Hell; they paint what they saw at Hiroshima after the dropping of the bomb.

That trend is also evident in *anime*, and probably for the same reason. Horror makes a better story than bliss. In *Judge*, for example, the underworld is guarded by an old hag who strips the dead of their remaining possessions. Even the relatively blameless dead are reduced to pathetic wraiths, mere shadows of what they were in life. The guilty dead face unknown horrors. And **Judge** presents a fairly traditional view of the afterlife drawn, more or less, from Buddhist traditions.

There are worse alternatives. In *Roots Search*, for example, Buzz and Moira battle an alien creature who claims to be a messenger from God. Whether or not this is true is never made clear. Moira refuses to believe it, but the creature's intimate knowledge of everyone's darkest, most deeply hidden secrets, and its tendency to make the punishment fit the crime are consistent with some Buddhist and Judeo-Christian views of God at his least lovable. God, according to the creature in *Roots Search*, is fed up with humanity and has condemned them all to death and Hell. Buzz and Moira fight back, and eventually die together in a suicide effort to save humanity by destroying their ship with the creature aboard. For them, death is not the end, however. They regain consciousness in a cavern that looks suspiciously like the beast's interior. The movie ends as they vow to face the unknown together, whether it be a glorious future or unspeakable horror. Their spirit is admirable, but given the *anime* universe, the odds are in favor of unspeakable horror.

Some views of the afterlife are drawn from neither Shinto nor Buddhism. **Night on the Galactic Railroad** offers several options in the form of stations along the way as two young friends embark on a mystical voyage from which only one will return. One station is drawn directly from Western traditions and features a glowing cross, white-robed pilgrims and a chorus singing "hallelujah." But the two heroes don't get off there. Perhaps that's because they aren't Christian. Their Heaven, it seems, is more personal. For one boy, it takes the form of a beautiful field where his mother awaits. The other sees only a black void in space, a coal sack. He can't disembark with his friend either. Even the best of friends can share only so much. At the end, death must be faced alone, and what comes next is still a mystery.

"Love Me Tender," the third episode of **Phantom Quest Corp.** also borrows from Western traditions, in this case, to produce a more light-hearted view of death. The ghost of Higashi Narita, a graduate student who died of exposure during an archeological expedition, first manifests in a classic Shinto/horror film form as a sundried mummy. As his story unfolds, however, he takes on a more human form as the earnest, bespectacled, slightly nerdish young man he was in life. He has remained on Earth to assist his one-time fiancée in mounting an exhibit of his life's work, and also in fending off the lecherous advances of a company executive who gives new meaning to the term sexual harassment. Once he has succeeded, he leaves the scene without any threats of exorcism. Conceding that a dead man is of no use to a living woman, he vows to watch over his fiancée from Heaven but to stay out of her life. He then sprouts Western-style wings and a halo, and floats upward out of the screen. The result is obviously not a serious attempt to persuade the audience of a Christian-style afterlife. It is simply a means to get rid of an unusually sympathetic spook in the kindest way possible. The fact that the author had to resort to Western symbols however, does indicate the fact that his own heritage lacks the ability to sugar-coat death quite so effectively.

That, of course, leads to a series of questions. If the Japanese view of death and the afterlife is so depressing, why do they focus on it so obsessively in a medium intended for amusement purposes? And, even more baffling, why are Americans who are raised with a much happier view of death and what follows it, so drawn to the bleak Japanese perspective?

The reason why the Japanese deal with death as they do is the easiest to explain. As has been discussed, death is much more a part of the heroic tradition in Japan where heroism is defined by motivation than it is in the West where heroism is more dependent on result. For the Japanese, death is the final proof of the hero's selflessness, of the purity and altruism of his motives. If he dies, and especially if that death is seen as permanent oblivion, no other motive is possible.

Death is also very much a part of Japan's literary and dramatic tradition of *mono no aware*, the idea that true beauty can be found only in impermanence. The constant awareness of death increases the appreciation of life both in reality and in fiction. That, in turn, ties back into the heroic tradition. This is summed up in Tsunetomo Yamamoto's famous dictum that "the way of the samurai is death," usually interpreted as meaning that a warrior must always be prepared to die. That meaning is definitely in there. However, anyone who reads the entire *Hagakure*, the work from which this well-known phrase is drawn, soon discovers that the author meant much more than that. He also meant that constant awareness of death improves the quality of life.

Mono no aware pervades many *anime* tear jerkers. It is the quality that makes **Grave of the Fireflies** so heart-breaking. A story about two children dying of starvation in the last days of World War II is sad by definition, but it is the small, precious moments of happiness in their lives that throw the tragedy into high relief. And, in turn, it is the knowledge that death is inevitable that makes those moments so unbearably bright and beautiful. The same is true of **Night on the Galactic Railroad**, a fantasy based on a 1927 literary classic. Two boys from a race of sentient cats find themselves aboard a strange train traveling toward an unknown destination. At first, they just enjoy the ride and the odd people they meet on the way. But later, as they begin to realize that everyone else on the train is dead, and that only one of them has a return ticket, the boys focus in on their friendship and the added value it gives to each remaining minute of their final voyage together. The boy who does return enunciates the lesson he has learned when he vows to make his life count, to burn brightly in the world for whatever time he has. Even Americans who have never heard of *mono no aware* or the way of the samurai understand the emotional beauty and meaning of these two *anime*.

A constant awareness of death also increases the tension. Because death is always possible in *anime*, cliff-hangers really hang. **Star Blazers** fans discovered that fact in the 1980s as the countdown to the end of the Earth progressed. Fans didn't just have to worry about what was going to happen to their favorite characters, they had to worry about whether or not the mission would succeed at all. After all, a show that would kill off its own heroes might just as easily do in the entire planet.

Maintaining dramatic tension is not the only attraction *anime*'s focus on death holds for American *otaku*, however. They are also attracted by the *mono no aware* elements of *anime*, even when they don't know what that is. They may be unaware of the long Japanese tradition that sees impermanence as the key to true beauty, but they do know that when an *anime* character dies, it leaves them with a different feeling than they get with most American films. *Anime* deaths often leave them feeling bad and good at the same time, and they like it.

American television is only just starting to realize that. Death made its American television debut on ***Star Trek: The Next Generation*** when Tasha Yar was eliminated by a living tarpit. Her death was very much in the *anime* style, unexpected, unjust, and ultimately pointless. That wasn't entirely accidental. A large number of the people associated with the ***Star Trek*** series are *otaku* and freely acknowledge their debt to the Japanese art form by including small *anime* in-jokes in the scripts.[7]

American television executives were obviously nervous about allowing death to make such an intimate appearance. The fact that one of the regulars was about to die was announced well in advance, presumably so that those viewers who might find it unduly upsetting could avoid watching. The only suspense left was which character was destined to meet the big D. A few episodes later, it seemed as if ***Star Trek*** had relented. Through a plot involving a time warp, Tasha Yar was brought back to die a more meaningful death. But later on it transpired that she hadn't even done that. She had lived through the original suicide mission, been captured, and forced to marry her Romulan captor. Eventually, she bore a half-Romulan daughter who not only killed her mother but went on to menace the Enterprise.

Even this revised fate of Tasha Yar was in the *anime* tradition. It was cruel, pointless, and utterly unfair. However, none of the ***Star Trek*** series have yet dared to repeat it. Whether it took the form of viewer protests or sponsor pressure, the American view of a moral universe has so far triumphed. That's a pity because ***Star Trek*** was definitely on the right track. Its older, Baby Boomer devotees may have been shocked, but younger fans would happily consign a few more regulars to an early grave, to be mourned and agonized over. That's what they love in *anime*. And it's what they don't get in American entertainment.

It's not just that American TV doesn't deal with the subject of death. American TV actively avoids it. So does every other aspect of American

[7]The sister ship of the *Enterprise,* for example, is the *Yamato*. In one episode, two smaller vessels named the *Yuri* and the *Kei* (the names of *anime*'s ***Dirty Pair***) make a brief appearance. In another episode, the calligraphy of background scrolls spells out the names of ***Urusei Yatsura's*** main characters.

society. Death is America's new obscenity, something you don't mention in public and especially something that must never be discussed in front of the young. The schools, worried by rising teen suicide rates, actively discourage texts and topics that might be deemed depressing. Book publishers and Disney studios alike seem determined to tag happy, death-free endings onto even time-honored classics like ***The Little Mermaid***.

Meanwhile, outside the controllable realm of fiction, death is a far more familiar companion to the young than their elders care to admit. Whether it comes in the form of AIDS, drug overdoses, car accidents, teen suicides, or gang-related shootings, death is very much a part of growing up in America. *Anime* may not be the best medium for beginning a serious discussion about death, but at least it's willing to talk about the subject. And it's willing to talk about it in a way that doesn't preach.

Sadly, the few American media attempts to deal with death, mourning, and the afterlife, movies like ***Ghost*** or TV series like ***Highway to Heaven*** or ***Touched by an Angel***, do preach. Eventually everything is resolved. The bad are punished and the good rewarded. The survivors are comforted by the knowledge that those they have lost have gone to a better place.

Most *otaku* complain that such movies aren't very realistic. What they really mean (since neither *anime* nor the American productions could be described as anything but fantasy), is that the American attempt to divide the dead into saints and sinners simply doesn't ring true. Generation X is sometimes described as being more cynical than earlier generations; it is certainly more aware of the fact that the good and evil in one personality is not so easy to separate. For that reason, many Gen-Xers also reject the idea of simple-minded reward and punishment on the Heaven-Hell model. Such a model actually offers little comfort to those whose friends have died from causes associated with activities Christianity considers sinful: drugs, AIDS, or drunk driving, for example. Those friends are still mourned, but any introduction of the Judeo-Christian model of Heaven and Hell leads to disconcerting questions about whether those friends really are in a better place.

By contrast, the amoral, indifferent universe of *anime* with its assumption that death means oblivion is positively encouraging. It also conforms to their view of life in general. Like every other generation, Gen-Xers draw their view of life from their personal experiences. They were born into an overcrowded world filled with crime, and informed that they would spend the rest of their life paying off debts they had not rung up. Most of them accept this with better grace than their elders have any right to expect, but most of them are also understandably cynical about the naturally moral universe implied by the neatly judgmental endings of American programming.

The subject needn't be as dramatic or as final as death. Other bad things happen to good people. They lose their innocence or their dreams. They suffer from unrequited love. They suffer physical or emotional traumas. Here too, Gen-Xers judge the *anime* approach to be more realistic. American TV and film writers provide tidy endings. Lost dreams and/or innocence are replaced by new ideals and goals. Rejected lovers learn to love again. Physical or emotional traumas are ameliorated through medical, psychiatric, or religious intervention. That seldom happens in *anime*. In *anime* some bad stuff never stops happening.

The most common case of bad stuff happening is mourning. Death may or may not finish things off for the hero, but there is usually someone left behind who cared. Some of them continue to care and to mourn for the rest of their lives. In ***Galaxy Express***, for example, a little boy sees his mother gunned down for sport by cyborg "human-hunters." Later, he meets a woman named Maytel who not only looks like his lost mother, but takes him in and cares for him throughout his adventures aboard an intergalactic train. In an American film, that would solve the problem. Another person has stepped in to replace the lost mother. Although the death of the original was undoubtedly a tragedy, the boy's need has been filled and he will be able to resume his interrupted childhood. Not in *anime*. Not even in an *anime* designed for children as ***Galaxy Express*** was.

In ***Galaxy Express,*** Maytel's motives are suspect and little Joey (Tetsuo in the Japanese original) quickly realizes this. More to the point, his reaction to her is not entirely filial. He is on the verge of adolescence and finds her distantly, impossibly desirable. He never mistakes her for his mother. His mother is dead and cannot be replaced. He continues to mourn her and to take what satisfaction he can in his new relationship with Maytel and the many other strange people he meets along the way. That, in fact, is the message of ***Galaxy Express:*** that we are all of us alone, that we will eventually lose everyone and everything we care about, and that we must therefore get the most we can out of every moment of life and love. It's a difficult lesson for a little boy to learn, but Joey manages. So do most *otaku*. Hollywood still hasn't caught on.[8]

[8]Actually, Hollywood may slowly be catching on. The film noir revival that has produced *Leaving Las Vegas, Pulp Fiction,* and *12 Monkeys* is a promising start, but it's still just a start.

Chapter Six

The fate of Yukari in **Doomed Megalopolis** is even less encouraging without causing any noticeable loss of popularity. **Doomed Megalopolis** focuses on the efforts of various mediums to exorcize Kato, a demon who is terrorizing 1920s Tokyo. Yukari's story is a related subplot. Yukari is an innocent schoolgirl who is particularly vulnerable to demonic possession. One medium suggests that this is probably due to some great trauma early in life. He wonders if she has had a close brush with death; according to him, Yukari has the look of one who has reached the gates of Hell and returned. Yukari's friends and relatives deny that she has experienced any such trauma, but the audience soon comes to know better. Yukari has been the victim of incestuous rape by her older brother ever since she reached puberty. That early trauma is compounded when she is possessed by the demon, raped by him as well, and finally forced to endure the shame of illegitimacy when she gives birth to an unwanted and possibly cursed child.

As a result of all these experiences, the once sweet-natured, intelligent schoolgirl becomes a hollow-eyed, snarling madwoman. Her fate has other victims too. The gentle student who loves her remains loyally by her side, growing older and sadder as he recognizes the impossibility of any real relationship with the woman Yukari has become. And then there is her illegitimate daughter, Yukiko, a strange child with unusual talents who may yet face a fate worse than that of her mother. Even when good has triumphed and Kato's evil has (sort of) been exorcized, these people's lives are still in ruins and there is little hope that anything will change that.

A similar theme of youthful loss and the end of innocence comes in **Green Legend Ran.** The young hero, Ran, lives in an environmentally destroyed future. In addition to the privations imposed by chronic shortages of food and water, Ran and his family must also endure raids by the Gestapo-like police of the Rodoists, a fanatical religious group that has succeeded in dominating the planet. Ran's mother was killed by the Rodoists and his father ran off to join the Hazzard, a resistance group. Predictably, Ran also leaves home to join the Hazzard and to find his father. What happens to him, however, is not so predictable. The Hazzard turns out to be considerably less heroic than young Ran imagined. The once courageous resistance group is corrupt and torn by factional divisions. Ran's father, too, is less than his son had hoped for.

Like any young man on a quest, Ran falls in love on the way. Aira, the girl he loves, is as idealistic as he is and doomed to similar disappointments. After being captured and tortured by the Rodoist church fathers, Aira manages to escape and make her way directly to the Holy Mother the Rodoists worship. The Holy Mother turns out to be a real deity, but she is neither benevolent nor honest. Although she does intend to restore Earth's environment, her reasons are her own and do not necessarily benefit humanity. When Aira realizes that she is necessary to the Holy Mother's plans, she attempts to bargain on behalf of the human race. Eventually, the Holy Mother agrees to spare humanity if Aira will sacrifice herself to the Holy Green, a group entity composed of girls like Aira which, when complete, will restore water and vegetation. Once the girl has done so, however, the goddess breaks her promise.

Ran and Aira both survive physically, but their ideals do not. By the end of the series, they are forced to admit that despite their efforts, the world is as terrible a place as it was when they started. Indeed, they may have made things worse. Their love for each other is all they have left and they use it to make a final promise to the future: to survive by whatever means necessary.

Not all bad stuff is so potentially lethal. There's always the first of life's little betrayals: unrequited love or, worse yet, the love triangle. Given that most *otaku* are in their late teens or early twenties, it's not surprising that romance is part of almost all *anime* regardless of what else is going on. The American media is not unaware of the lure of romance either, of course, but there, too, American popular depictions shy away from the less attractive aspects. In particular, American shows about love shy away from triangular relationships in which friendship and love collide. Those triangles that do appear on American television are usually fairly clear-cut. Two people vie for the affections of a third. Two of them are fairly sympathetic. One is not. If the two sympathetic people wind up together, all's well. If not, the one left out makes a new life for him or herself, and the lover who chose wrongly soon realizes that fact. Either way, you don't have to feel sorry for anyone.

It's a pity that life isn't that tidy, but it isn't and *anime* recognizes that. In series such as **Kimagure Orange Road**, for example, it's not just a question of two girls, Madoka and Hikaru, fighting over a boy, Kyōsuke. The girls are close friends, bound together by Hikaru's dependence on Madoka, and Madoka's feelings of responsibility toward Hikaru. They grew up together, and theirs is also a *sempai-kōhai* relationship with all the implications of responsibility and trust that carries. Because of friendship, Madoka regularly stands back and helps Hikaru in her efforts to interest Kyōsuke. Unfortunately, Kyōsuke is actually more interested in Madoka. And, although Madoka fights against it, she loves Kyōsuke in return. You don't have to be terribly experienced in love to understand that however this situation gets resolved, someone is going to be seriously hurt.

Similar stories of unrequited love abound in **Ranma ¹/₂.** The ambiguity of Ranma and Akane's relationship, combined with the fact that they are both attractive people, means that they frequently attract the attention of other people. Mostly such extraneous attachments are played for laughs, but not always. Even Ryōga, Akane's hopeless, hapless admirer, is allowed a few moments of dignity. Throughout most of the series, Ryōga is a natural butt for all jokes. He has such a poor sense of direction that he can barely find his way around the block, and when splashed with cold water, he turns into a piglet. His efforts to take Akane away from Ranma are doomed to failure, and eventually he comes to realize that. There is a lot of comic potential in Ryōga's efforts to adjust to that realization, but Takahashi doesn't exploit them. Instead, the episode in which Ryōga helps Akane to train for an important fight is genuinely touching. There's comedy too, but Ryōga is not the butt.

Of course, both **Kimagura Orange Road** and **Ranma ¹/₂** are comedies. That means that although unrequited love may be played for pathos, it never really becomes tragic. That's not the case in all *anime.* **Macross Plus** takes a more serious approach to the same theme as **Kimagure Orange Road**, childhood friends whose friendship is threatened by romantic rivalry. In **Macross Plus**, however, the friends are older and meaner. The gender ratio is reversed too, two men and one woman. It doesn't help that the two men are test pilots for U.N. Spacy, or that they control huge robotic war machines, or that one of them, Guld, is only half human and has questionable control over his temper, or that underneath it all, they love each other. It also doesn't help that Myung, the young woman, actually loves both of them in different ways, or that she's having a career crisis, or that a virtual reality singing idol has misinterpreted her feelings as an order to destroy the Earth. By the end of **Macross Plus**, it is obvious that the situation cannot continue and that one of the two men must die. One does.

The way in which *anime* treats love is similar to the way it treats any other subject. The fact that a happy ending is possible doesn't mean that that's what's going to happen. Some eternal triangles do resolve themselves, but others don't. Sometimes the resolution is worse than the original dilemma. In some cases, all three parties may go their separate ways so that nobody gets to be happy. Happy endings are still fairly common. Everyone likes to see young lovers win out. But the fact that their victory is not guaranteed adds dramatic value.

And that, perhaps, is the real reason Americans, like Japanese, enjoy death and all the other bad stuff in *anime*. It's not just that *anime* deals with dilemmas in a more realistic fashion, or that it raises issues considered taboo in America. *Anime*'s willingness to show death and bad stuff restores a kind of tension, a genuine dramatic emotionality that Hollywood and network TV seem to have forgotten about.

And *anime* presents these unpleasant realities in a pleasant guise. That, after all, is one purpose of entertainment, to allow us to look at things in a new way. However, such subjects as death, loss, and even first love are often too painful to bring out into the light of day. *Anime* portrays them in a way that does not disguise their true nature, but renders them bearable. That's partly because of the artificial nature of the medium which has a natural distancing effect. However, *anime* has another advantage when it comes to making disturbing subjects bearable. Because of its Japanese origin, *anime* can draw on centuries of a literary tradition devoted to bringing beauty out of pain. This is the tradition of *mono no aware*, the belief that something is beautiful because it is transient and will soon be lost. Young Americans, who have already lost a lot and look to losing even more in the future, find that an attractive idea.

Chapter Seven

Outrageous Women

Who you gonna call?

- when the shadows in your bedroom have eyes and teeth?
- when the universe is threatened with extinction?
- when robots are running amok in the streets of Tokyo?
- when your best friend's been kidnaped by an insane sorcerer?
- when your ex-wife has decided to settle the child custody issue with a laser-cannon?

Who you gonna call? A woman, that's who.

In the world of *anime*, women are as likely to play the hero as men. That often comes as a surprise to new fans who assume that *anime* will reflect the low status of women in Japanese society. In fact, that assumption is based on two erroneous premises. The first erroneous idea is that *anime* reflects contemporary Japanese society as it really is or even as Japanese animators would like it to be. The second is that Japanese women are far more oppressed than their American counterparts. Neither is true.

Anime deliberately focuses on the bizarre, the fantastic. And in Japan, as in America, ratings and sales statistics do matter. That is nowhere more apparent than in the way women are portrayed in *anime*. They may be heroes or villains, saints or sinners, but they rarely blend into the background. And they rarely wear much in the way of clothing. It would be easy to dismiss this as pure sexual fantasy for male (and perhaps a few female) *otaku*. It's more than that.[1]

[1]Except, of course, in the case of pure pornography. This is a small portion of the Japanese *anime* market which is disproportionately represented in America.

One reason strong, sexy women are so prevalent in *anime* is because they attract a wide audience. Men will watch because of the sex and women will watch because of the strength, or so the popular wisdom goes. Actually, a good story line, solid characters, and creative animation have a lot more to do with drawing an audience than even the briefest bikini. But there's no doubt that sex helps sell a show in America and Japan.

Unfortunately, simply wanting to create strong, sexy women is not enough. American cartoonists, authors, and script writers have been trying to do that for years. With a very few exceptions, they seldom succeed in producing anything believable.

That's partly because the Western tradition contains far fewer models to work from. Despite the efforts of feminists, politically correct scholars, and avant garde theologians, Western gods, heroes, and other idols remain predominantly male, and that fact is reflected in the popular culture. Fantasy fiction gets around this problem by reaching back to a pagan past, but it has to reach a long way back. And even then, creating believably strong women is difficult because of the actual position of women in contemporary Western society.

Anime faces the same problems, but not so dramatically. Contemporary Japanese religious and secular traditions include far more women in dominant roles than Western traditions ever did. And, despite some setbacks in the nineteenth century, contemporary Japanese women continue to uphold much of that tradition in real life.

Contrary to the belief of most Americans, Japanese women are not necessarily any more oppressed than American women. They aren't necessarily any less oppressed either. They are simply oppressed in different ways. The nature of that oppression is not static in either society. Moreover, the role of women is changing rapidly and dramatically in both Japan and America. In both countries, too, the media tends to focus on the changes and to ignore women's more traditional roles.

That's a pity, because Japanese women's main strength still lies in their traditional role, a stark contrast to the position of women in America. American women undeniably have greater access to positions of political and economic power, but the fate of American women who choose more traditional roles as wives and mothers is far from enviable. Most American housewives would never even dream of asking for the kind of power their Japanese counterparts take for granted. Traditional Japanese women control the family budget, keep their husbands on strict allowances, determine most major purchases, and have the majority voice in how their children are reared and educated. Under some circumstances, they not only keep their own names, but also bestow it on their husbands and children. Moreover, Japanese women derive considerable prestige from performing their traditional roles in a satisfactory way. This is not simply a matter of social approbation; these women often play a major role in local (and sometimes not so local) politics.

The details of those lives are seldom shown in *anime* for the same reason that the details of a businessman's life are seldom shown. Both are dull. (Takahashi did her best to try to make something of Kasumi's kitchen in **Ranma ¹/₂**, but eventually even she gave up on the project.) *Anime* does, however, devote some time to the practical, emotional, and intellectual rewards of traditional women's roles.

Unfortunately, the best reflection of attitudes toward traditional women's roles is found in pure *shōjo* (girls') *manga*, few of which ever make it into *anime* or translation. Although these focus primarily on romance and courtship, they do reveal a lot about the seriousness with which contemporary Japanese girls regard marriage and its responsibilities. Some hint of those attitudes can be found in **Maison Ikkoku** as Kyōko considers her future as a young widow. Although she is financially and socially secure in that role, she obviously finds it less than satisfying. Sex and romance play their role in encouraging her to try again for fulfillment in marriage, but so do the social pressures and incentives that surround her on a daily basis.

In **They Were 11**, a science fiction *anime* created by a well-established *shōjo manga* artist, Hagio Moto, marriage and motherhood are taken seriously as alternatives to more traditionally male career ambitions as an androgynous alien, Frol, tries to decide which sex to become. The earthman who loves Frol hopes s/he will choose to become a woman, but Frol must consider gender roles and lifestyle options as well as love in making her/his choice. Eventually, Frol gets to have her cake and eat it too, but her internal debate is revealing.

The prestige Japanese women derive from their traditional role is also evident in *anime* clearly intended for men and boys. **The Venus Wars**, for example, is typical of male-oriented science fiction *anime*. The hero is Hiro Seno, a handsome young motorcycle racer who becomes embroiled in a war between two colonies on the planet Venus. The fact that this is drawn from *shōnen* (boys') *manga* does not preclude strong female characters from supporting roles. In fact, **The Venus Wars** includes two very feisty young women. There's Miranda, a motorcycle-riding warrior woman, as tough and gutsy as any man but a lot sexier. And there's Susan Somers, an ambitious career journalist with more than her fair share of charm. Yet, in the end, Hiro falls for neither Susan nor Miranda. Instead, he turns to Margo, a sweetly traditional young woman.

That might be seen as a typical example of male chauvinism but, as is so often the case with *anime*, there's a trick. The fact is that Hiro finds Margo only moderately attractive as a sweetly vulnerable young girl whose interests revolve around fashion and the shopping mall. The two become serious only after Hiro is seriously wounded and crawls to her for help. And only at the end of the movie, when the war is lost and he finds her in a refugee camp struggling valiantly to hold together her shattered family, does he realize the full extent of his feelings for her. He loves her not because she is a vulnerable child who needs his care, but because he finally realizes that behind the girlish façade there is a strong maternal woman who will take care of him.

Margo is a warrior's woman rather than a warrior woman. She seems compliant, but in fact she is extremely self-reliant. She assures her warrior that when the battle is over, he will still have a home to come home to. She regards this as her duty more than her right, although is also an act of love. And Margo has not really reached the height of her power. She will achieve that only when she becomes a mother and head of her own family.

Margo is an admirable figure. Not all Japanese women in traditional roles come off so well. Maternal strength takes on a nightmarish form in **Roujin Z**, Katsuhiro Ōtomo's nightmarish fantasy about a life support system gone berserk. The real trouble begins when an experimental robotic hospital bed takes on the personality of the patient's dead

1. In *anime*, eyes are used to convey a character's feelings. Sensitive characters have larger eyes than insensitive ones. Sasami, the only person in **Tenchi Muyō!** who even seems to care about how anyone else feels, has enormous eyes.

2. As might be expected in a country where most of the population has black hair, that color usually has positive connotations. When Ranma of *Ranma 1/2* is splashed with cold water, he becomes a she. In addition to the expected physical changes, his hair color changes from black to red. This not only serves to differentiate the two personas, but also gives a color coded cue as to which is the true, the proper Ranma.

3. Osamu Tezuka is sometimes called the Walt Disney of Japan. Tezuka was influenced by Disney as a young man, but his later work took an entirely different direction. Given the similarities between Disney Studio's *The Lion King* and Tezuka's earlier work, *Kimba the White Lion,* perhaps Disney should be called the Osamu Tezuka of America.

4. Americans can enjoy a series like ***Urusei Yatsura*** as pure slapstick, but an appreciation of the way in which the artist has blended Japanese history, literature, mythology, and popular culture is part of the fun of really good *anime*. In ***Urusei Yatsura,*** the popular Shinto-Taoist goddess, Benten, is portrayed as a biker babe.

5. Oyuki, a ghostly creature drawn from Shinto folklore, becomes the Princess of Neptune. She's less lethal in this guise, but her need for snow shovelers and her penchant for sherbert can still cause plenty of trouble.

6. Technically, Lum of ***Urusei Yatsura*** fulfills the traditional description of an *oni,* the demons of Japanese folklore. She has horns, oddly colored hair, supernatural powers and wears tiger skins. She's not as large and ugly as the traditional *oni* and she doesn't eat people, but when she gets angry, look out!

7. It's often hard to tell the gods from the demons in *anime*. That's especially true in a series like **Vampire Princess Miyu** where the heroine's pretty face and hair ribbons hide her eerie nature.

8. Sometimes it's even hard to tell good from evil in *anime*. In this episode of ***Vampire Princess Miyu***, Miyu tries to save a schoolboy from a demon, seemingly a worthy goal. But Miyu's motives are often mixed. In this case, she wants the boy for her own pleasures.

9. Ayaka Kisaragi, President of **Phantom Quest Corporation,** is a *miko,* for the nineties. She's still pretty good at exorcizing demons, but she doesn't live in a shrine or dress traditionally, and she feels free to spend her money on her three hobbies: shopping, drinking and *karaoke.*

10. In *Oh, My Goddess!* the three norns of Norse tradition, Verthandi, Urd, and Skuld, find themselves living in Tokyo. They also seem to have acquired a Buddhist-style third eye since leaving their native fjords.

11. Shiro Lhadatt of ***The Wings of Honneamise*** is an alienated young man searching for meaning in a corrupt and cynical world. He finally finds it in the cold, clear purity of space and his own heart. That makes him an ideal hero for the nineties, but in fact, Shiro's concept of heroism is drawn from quite ancient Japanese traditions.

12. Historical *anime* often do poorly in the United States because they demand a grasp of Japanese history few Americans possess. ***The Dagger of Kamui*** does better than most partly because much of it plays in America, but mostly because it deals with an obscure facet of Japanese history and with a minority group in northern Japan called the Ainu. This means Japanese audiences also need a lot of explanations which are included in the script.

13. ***Ninja Scroll,*** which is more fantasy than history, also goes down well with American audiences.

14. ***Astro Boy*** was the first mecha ever to get a green card. He first appeared on American television in 1964. Together with his robot family, he taught us that machines had feelings too.

15. Most *anime* robots are really exoskeletal suits which rely on one or more human pilots to guide them. They can be little more than a light-weight outfit like the powersuits of the Knight Sabers in ***Bubblegum Crisis/ Bubblegum Crash.***

16. Or they can be huge, transforming space ships like the **Gunbuster**.

© 1988 Victor/Gainax/B.M.D.

© Hikari Productions/Amuse Video/Plex/Atlantis

17. **Giant Robo** represents the ultimate in retro-*mecha*. Not only is Robo a barrel-like construct of nuts, bolts, and meshing gears, but its young pilot, Daisaku, must ride on the outside, either in **Giant Robo**'s hand or hanging onto a ladder that runs up the robot's head. He controls the robot with a wristwatch radio, complete with antenna, no less!

18. Death and misery are two surprisingly popular features of *anime*. Gally, the heroine of **Battle Angel** is an indestructible cyborg. However, her strength simply means that she will survive to mourn the deaths of those she loves.

19. Female bonding is a major theme in many "girls with guns" *anime*. In **Bubblegum Crisis/Bubblegum Crash,** the relationships between the Knight Sabers are every bit as important to the series' popularity as the *mecha*.

20. Keiichi Morisato of **Oh, My Goddess!** is typical of the passive males often found in fantasy *anime*. So far from resenting Belldandy's powers, he seems quite content to be overshadowed by his goddess.

wife, Haru. Like many traditional Japanese wives, Haru expressed her love for her husband by mothering him. Revived as a robotic version of herself, she is not only strong but gentle, patient, and self-sacrificing in her misguided attempt to fulfill her dying, confused husband's wish to spend a day with her on the beach at Kamakura. Her soft, wheedling voice combined with a powerful *mecha* body leaves the audience in no doubt that things will not end well. And they don't.

The long-suffering and/or controlling Japanese mother pervades the Japanese media. Her image, similar in many ways to that of the Jewish mother in America, is not altogether flattering. She is extolled in maudlin songs by drunken *salarimen*[2] and reviled for her excessive focus on her children's education. Her children alternatively love and fear her. So does her husband. So does Japanese public opinion. Such is the price of power.

In the world of *anime*, however, mothers are more often remarkable for their absence. This is because *anime*, especially *anime* about the young, is aimed at the young, or at those who prefer to remember their youth in a cloud of nostalgia. That means remembering it without the strong, controlling hand of a true Japanese mother getting in the way.

Anime artists recognize that need, sometimes very explicitly. Takahashi has great fun pointing out the difference between her portrayals of ridiculously angst-ridden, hormonally disadvantaged teens and the usual, idealized media version. In the first Ranma movie, for example, the word *"Seishun"* (the springtime of youth) backed by the rays of the rising sun appears above the head of Kuno, who is not only striking a pose, but obviously leading the entire gang toward sheer disaster. Even Takahashi, however, stops short of introducing a maternal figure unless she absolutely has to. In **Ranma ¹/₂**, Ranma's mother is absent most of the time, and the Tendo girls' mother is conveniently dead. That's vital to the whole mood of **Ranma ¹/₂**. The presence of a strong, responsible mother would kill all the fun.

That fact was made manifest in the "Whose Kitchen Is It, Anyway?" episode of **Ranma ¹/₂** when Ranma's mother at last makes an appearance, and shows everyone why Takahashi had to kill off the Tendo girls' mother before even beginning the series. As long as the Tendo household was composed of two fathers, one son and three daughters, chaos and misunderstandings, the very foundations of comedy, are only to be expected. With the arrival of Mrs. Saotome, all that

[2]Japanese businessmen, best known in this country for their acumen and work ethic. Better known to their compatriots as a wretched pack of overworked economic animals whose main release is drink and karaoke in hostess bars.

disappears. Although her husband and son hide from her by remaining in their cursed forms (as a panda and a girl respectively), she nonetheless manages to restore harmony and order. If there's anything a comedy like **Ranma ¹/₂** doesn't need, it's harmony and order.

This, more than misogyny, probably accounts for the large number of dead mothers in *anime*. Death is often preferable to what they can expect if they stick around. Mothers do better if they simply don't appear at all. If they do appear, they run the risk of being denigrated to the level of the Japanese media's lowest figure of fun: the father figure. This is what happens to Ataru's mother in **Urusei Yatsura**. Ataru's father, a nerve-shattered wreck who spends most of his home life cowering behind his newspaper, is a very typical portrayal of a Japanese father not only in *anime* but also in live-action dramas and often even in novels. In most other forms of entertainment, his weak role would be balanced by a strong maternal role. In an *anime* comedy like **Urusei Yatsura**, however, balance is the last thing anyone wants. As a result, Mrs. Moroboshi, too, is a broken creature reduced to casting despairing glances at her demon-ridden son and whimpering "I never should have had him."

Being absent or weak aren't an *anime* mother's only options, however. She can be personally strong provided she gives up her traditional role and becomes a career woman. Unfortunately, this may let her in for an even worse time. Although women with families and careers are increasingly common in Japan, Japanese society still has mixed feelings about them. Career mothers are popular in *anime* comedies partly because their lives don't give them the time to reduce all to order like a traditional mother, but also because they themselves become figures of fun.

This is exemplified in a series like **All-Purpose Cultural Cat Girl Nuku-Nuku** which focuses on the custody battle over a young boy, Ryunnosuke. Custody battles are no fun under any circumstances, and Ryunnosuke's circumstances are worse than most. He has been placed in the custody of his father, a brilliant but distinctly loony scientist. Unfortunately, his mother is the megalomaniacal president of an arms corporation, and willing to use all the weapons at her disposal in her efforts to retrieve her son. The series begins when one of his parents' battles costs the life of the boy's pet, a kitten named Nuku Nuku. His father immediately transplants the cat's brain into the body of a powerful robot with the outward appearance of a pretty teen-age girl. The result is an ultimate weapon who can be easily distracted by a ball of string. When Nuku-Nuku weighs in on the male side of the struggle, she changes the balance of power. Akiko, Ryunnosuke's mother, responds by becoming increasingly outrageous. She is a caricature of a career woman, too busy to spend much time with her son, but wildly possessive all the same.

It would be easy to dismiss portrayals like that of Akiko as mere misogyny and a blanket condemnation of all women who try to balance family and career. Certainly misogyny is part of the humor in ***All-Purpose Cultural Cat Girl Nuku-Nuku***, but even in a lightweight, slapstick comedy like this, the message is more complex. Yūzō Takada, the series' creator, does see a conflict between women having a career and children. However, he also points up some problems with women's traditional roles in the second episode when Akiko does, briefly, try to become an ordinary woman. Not only is she miserable in such a role, but she's bad at it, and the time taken up by domestic chores leaves her with less time than ever to spend with her son. Moreover, her ex-husband not only takes unfair advantage of her temporary subservience, but seems oddly bored by her in this role. As the series progresses, it also becomes apparent that Akiko is deeply loved by both her son and her ex-husband, not in spite of her outrageous behavior, but because of it. This is a family comedy that plays on the problems caused by working mothers, but it stops short of being an outright condemnation.

Certainly *anime* does not condemn career women generally. Careers are fine for single, childless women. Indeed, in futuristic science fiction *anime*, they're almost required. This is because Japanese, like Americans, tend to assume that greater gender equality is part of progress. Even so, the Japanese have been bolder in including women fully in their science fiction. The presence of Lisa Hayes (Misa Hayase), a strong young woman, in a command position was one of the features that made ***Robotech*** so popular in America in the early 1980s.

The Japanese are, perhaps, more comfortable with the idea because their own past and legends contain more female heroes. Also, the separate development of girls' (*shōjo*) *manga* in postwar Japan meant that one whole genre featured women in leading roles regardless of what went on in the rest of Japanese society. Certainly *anime* science fiction has been faster to introduce high-ranking women into its space program than American television. Long before ***Star Trek: Voyager*** took the plunge with Captain Janeway, Captain Soundy sailed the galaxies with an all-female crew in ***Gall Force***. Indeed, Kate Mulgrew's original portrayal of Captain Janeway was suspiciously like Captain Soundy right down to her hair style.

But not all *anime* women of the future are in command positions, and not all *anime* futures are so welcoming to women. *Anime* like **Patlabor, A.D. Police, Appleseed**, and **New Dominion Tank Police**, for example, see women's roles as increasing, but not by much. All feature women as active, front-line members of the police, but they seem to be isolated. Their comrades are nearly all male. In **Bubblegum Crisis/Bubblegum Crash**, the A.D. Police are still very much a patriarchal organization. Nene Romanov may work for them, but her work is confined to clerical chores and traffic detail. Her real effectiveness, such as it is, is outside the system, as a member of a freelance, mercenary group, the Knight Sabers.

Even in the *anime* future, women do better in counterculture or non-mainstream operations. That's not usually because they don't want to contribute to their society, but because they doubt they will be allowed to do so in male-run institutions. Sometimes they don't seem to have much respect for how those organizations work either. Despite their claim to be in it for the money, the Knight Sabers of **Bubblegum Crisis/Bubblegum Crash**, are actually quite dedicated crime fighters. Priss is openly contemptuous of the A.D. Police, and the attitude of the others suggests that they, too, believe they can do a better job than the (male) authorities.

The same is true of **Armitage III**. At the beginning of the series, the protagonist, Naomi Armitage, still operates as a member of the Mars Police, albeit a fairly independent member. As time passes however, she becomes increasingly independent until she winds up as a fugitive from the organization she once served. That's partly because she begins to identify more and more with the fact that she is a "third," a third-generation robot. In **Armitage III**, however, robots exemplify the low position of women in Martian society. There are no human female characters except for a few brief shots of Earth's ruler who is middle-aged, unattractive, and corrupt. Most of the robots in **Armitage III** are subservient and a bit silly. They are sex toys, pantyless stewardesses, compliant concubines, and giggly newsgirls. They have metal buttons on the sides of their heads that allow men to turn them off if they become tiresome. Mars, as one character notes, is not a feminist society. The exceptions to all this are Armitage and her fellow "thirds." They are all female except for the last to come off the assembly line, and he is a prepubescent boy who can never age. The purpose of the "thirds" is as sexist as you can get. They were designed as breeders. They are robots who can reproduce, presumably in concert with a human male. The "thirds," however, have other ideas. They are intensely creative women: singers, artists, writers, and the like. They have made lives for themselves. They are also all single. This leaves them with only one problem. Their creator is trying to kill them and, for the most part, he succeeds. Armitage survives but ultimately succumbs to love and maternity in a remarkably sappy ending that bears little relationship to the rest of the series, except as evidence that trying to live outside the dominant patriarchy obviously didn't work for the "thirds" of Mars.

In Japan, women tend to go around sexist institutions rather than to confront them. Some careers, including those related to *manga* and *anime*, are more welcoming to women than others. However, the real bastions of power in both government and business are still predominantly male. Women in high places are increasing, but they are usually isolated, lone women in a sea of men. Early *anime* series like **Star Blazers** and **Robotech** never bothered to consider that point. Nova (Yuki Mori) and Lisa Hayes (Misa Hayase) never seemed troubled by the fact that they were surrounded only by men. As the number of real women in power increases in Japan, however, *anime* reflects a different situation. Chief Nagumo, the policewoman who takes on a corrupt department in **Patlabor 2** is a case in point. An early encounter with her former classmates, all male, from the police academy sets the mood. The men greet her cheerfully enough and congratulate her on her recent promotion. They even invite her to join them for drinks, but she declines. As she walks away, one of the men remarks that she probably doesn't want to meet Tsuge, their former teacher, because she had an affair with him while at the academy. He adds that for all her talent as a police officer, she is still plagued with a woman's heart. It's a minor incident, but it does point up that despite her high position, Nagumo's sex holds her apart from her colleagues. Later, when a corrupt city government starts looking for scapegoats, Nagumo learns just how dangerous gender isolation can be.

And Chief Nagumo has already reached a position of power. Other *anime* reveal many of the problems lower level women face as they strive to compete in business. Sexual harassment and office affairs are the most common. In one episode of **Phantom Quest Corp.**, a young woman is literally told that her prized job is contingent upon sleeping with the company president. Her predicament not only enrages her, but arouses a sisterly anger in Ayaka Kisaragi who brings her supernatural powers into play against the offending CEO. *Judge* offers a more balanced view of sex and the office. A sleazy, manipulative affair between an ambitious executive and the female clerk who aids him in embezzlement ends in her suicide and his death at the hands of the *Judge*. However, the warm, affectionate affair between the hero and his co-worker is what allows him to make the psychic connections that ultimately save the day.

Still, it's not surprising that many ambitious women prefer to strike out on their own as entrepreneurs, instead of dealing with the risky relationships, female-track jobs, and glass ceilings of the male establishment. In fact, that is what is happening in Japan which now sports a number of companies that are as solidly female as the establishment is male.

That reality is also mirrored even in the off-duty lives of the main characters in **Bubblegum Crisis/Bubblegum Crash**. Aside from their participation in the Knight Sabers, Priss, Linna, Silia, and Nene have jobs. Except for Nene, who uses her position within the A.D. Police to provide the others with information, none have chosen mainstream careers. Priss and Linna freelance in the relatively female-friendly spheres of entertainment and the health and fitness industry. Even the wealthy Silia Stingray whose career is more of a cover than a means of making a living, runs a lingerie boutique.

For the most part, the American women's movement rejected that separate-but-equal approach to economic and political life long ago. Although tactics differ, most women's groups have taken a confrontational approach. Their aim is to make mainstream establishments more accessible to women and more responsive to their needs. Initially, that approach was successful. Young women who enter the work force or the political arena in America today do not face the outright rejection and discrimination that their mothers faced. What they do face, however, is a more subtle form of discrimination, a long series of smaller inequities and put-downs that withhold earned rewards, and eat away at self-confidence and self-esteem. Moreover, after years of enforced consciousness raising on the social front, many young women are more at ease in the company of other women than their mothers. And many of them are beginning to reconsider the advantages of building all-female establishments rather than fighting it out day after day in power structures that remain basically patriarchal. At any rate, they are intrigued by the possibilities of the all-woman groups that they see in *anime*.

All of these futures assume that humanity will not blow itself up in some cataclysmic war or find some other way making this lush, green planet uninhabitable. Like their American counterparts, some Japanese aren't that optimistic. Some *anime* portray future dystopias in which all social order is gone, and in which human beings have reverted to their most basic instincts. Those future dystopias are often ugly places for women. Yet, exceptional women flourish even there. The worst of these future dystopias is probably the best known, at least among Americans: the world of **Akira**. In a world devastated by science run amok and managed by a scientific elite unconcerned with social needs, the streets are ruled by motorcycle gangs to whom women are little more than property. In one memorable scene, one gang member beats up another's girlfriend in order to send a message. Yet even there, one woman stands out from the rest. Throughout **Akira**, the resistance fighter Kay holds her own, not only because she is tougher and meaner than the men, but also because she never quite loses her idealism or her faith in the future.

The spirit world provides women with even more scope in supernatural or horror *anime*. Female mediums, priestesses, and magical girls abound in *anime*. That's an outgrowth of Shinto tradition and Japanese history. Queen Himiko, Japan's first known ruler, was a shaman, a mystic who spoke to the gods and who ruled in their name. She was the first, but she was not the only one. Later empresses like Jingū and Jitō who reigned in the third and seventh centuries respectively, followed the same tradition.[3] Although they did not rule alone as Himiko did, they were no mere adjuncts to a male ruler. They were co-rulers, the spiritual arm of a religious state. When their husbands died, they became female emperors and ran both sides of the government. When Jingū's husband died in battle because he ignored her predictions, she used her magic to postpone her pregnancy for over a year while she donned men's clothing and led her troops to victory. Jitō was less warlike, but a superb diplomat who united the feuding tribes of Japan into a single state loyal to the imperial family.

[3]Some scholars think Himiko and Jingū may have been the same person.

The age of female emperors officially ended in the eighth century, although some imperial women have occupied the throne since then in exceptional situations. However, the shamanistic tradition continued in the form of Shinto priestesses called *miko*. Until the 1930s *miko* were oracles. They danced themselves into a trance and then spoke with the voices of gods. They were banned by the militarists in the 1930s on the grounds that they made Japan look foolish and superstitious to others. Actually, they were an unpredictable and uncontrollable aspect of Shinto which the militarists were using for propaganda purposes. *Miko* have been making a comeback since the end of World War II. They dance again at most Shinto festivals and sometimes perform important rituals. Prophecies are still rare, but a number of women have founded new religions using some form of shamanistic talent.[4] But the real place to find *miko* in Japanese society today is in the world of *anime*.

That's not to say that they necessarily get any respect. *Urusei Yatsura*'s Miss Sakura is undeniably a *miko*. She identifies herself as such, operates out of a shrine, and wears the distinctive red *hakama* with a white top. Her powers are quite real, but not as well controlled as she thinks. In her first effort to exorcize Ataru, she succeeds instead in ridding herself of the demons that have ruined her health. Later results are even less useful although equally accidental. Miss Sakura is occasionally able to exorcize a demon, but she's equally likely to call one up.

[4] In keeping with Japanese tradition, these new religions are syncretic. Some identify themselves as Shinto or partly Shinto. Others do not.

Most *anime miko* do better than that. Chiaki, the heroine of *Zenki*, for example, controls a demon lord, Zenki, and uses him to fight evil. In his fighting form, *Zenki* is a fearsome creature and would cheerfully slaughter Chiaki along with the evil possession beasts he destroys in each episode. But, of course, he never gets the chance. Chiaki may still be in high school, but she is already a powerful *miko*. She controls *Zenki* by reducing him to a toddler: a demon still, but a baby demon who she then terrorizes and bullies like an older sister. In doing so, she also reveals how traditional Japanese women control the men in their lives. They turn them into children. Spoiled, pampered children to be sure, but children nonetheless, and as children, controllable. More recently, Japanese career women have begun to show a tendency to do the same thing in the public arena. Chiaki's method of controlling *Zenki* may seem funny to American women, but it's also very effective and something upwardly mobile young women might like to consider.

Nami Yamigumo, the only fully Japanese member of futuristic Tokyo's A.M.P. (Attack Mystification Police) force in *Silent Möbius*, was also a *miko* before she joined. She was trained by her grandfather, and only permitted to strike out on her own after she had proved her powers in a grueling initiation ritual.

Keiko, the *miko* who rids 1920s Tokyo of its demon in *Doomed Megalopolis* is undoubtedly the most powerful representative of this

Shinto tradition. Yet, Keiko is not really typical. That's not because the goddess she serves turns out to be Kannon, a Buddhist deity. Such eclecticism is common, and Kannon in particular has so merged with local traditions as to become at least as much a Shinto deity as a Buddhist one. However, Keiko marries into the Tatsumiya family as part of her campaign against Kato. That means not only that she loses her virginity, but also that she takes on responsibilities of a housewife.

In theory, a *miko* should be a virgin and remain aloof from such everyday cares as washing the dishes and preparing meals, to say nothing of bearing and raising children. In practice, since Shinto shrines are often hereditary, some *miko* are actually the wives of priests. *Anime* reflects that changed reality considerably better than many serious works on the subject of Shinto which often continue to insist that all *miko* are young and unmarried.

Still, most *anime miko* are young girls, and in most cases their powers are more related to heredity than training. Moreover, that heredity is almost always along the female line. This idea is most clearly found in the *manga, Mai: The Psychic Girl*. Mai Mihiro is unaware of her heritage until she receives a visit from her dead mother who evokes the memory of the countless generations of Mihiro women who have protected their people from evil. They appear behind her as a tableau of bare-breasted women standing side by side until they disappear into the mists of time. When Mai finally makes her stand against war and the male military establishment, she, too, goes in bare-breasted. Those breasts are more than mere titillation. They are a link with Mai's ancestors and also a symbol of the source of her power: her womanhood.

That's womanhood, not girlhood. The emergence of a *miko*'s powers are usually linked to puberty. Lan Komatsuzaki of **Blue Sonnet**, for example, owes her powers partly to her descent from an ancient line of demigods, but also to her sex. Her younger brother shares her ancestry, but he only begins to develop powers after a blood transfusion from his sister and he never reaches her level. Even Lan remains an ordinary girl until the day she begins to menstruate, an event that begins with cramps on the tennis courts and a thin stream of blood flowing down the drain in the gym showers, and ends with emergence of a new heroine: the Red Fang.

Not all transformations are so explicitly linked to biology. Sometimes the transformation is preceded simply by a comment on the heroine's age or the fact that her breasts are developing. For Miki, the heroine of **Zeguy**, the tip-off is her growing interest in boys, an interest that leads to a fight with her best friend at the beginning of the story. Miki is not even aware of the fact that she is an hereditary *miko*. She owes her powers to a long dead and forgotten ancestor, another *miko* known simply as the Shamas. Even so, Miki's powers do not manifest until she actually falls in love and sees her beloved in danger. Then, with a little help from a cat, she transforms into the white-clad Shamas, flies into the air, and rescues the man of her dreams.

Demon Hunter Yohko owes her powers to a combination of puberty and virginity, although in her case the latter is not always voluntary. Yohko is the 109th demon hunter of her line. She comes by that naturally. Her grandmother was the 108th. Her mother missed her chance because she lost her virginity before her powers had fully developed. Yohko's granny is determined that that won't happen again. She keeps a close eye on her granddaughter and, in one episode, actually drags the embarrassed, naked girl out from under her childhood sweetheart. Granny is no prude. Once Yohko's powers are fully developed, she urges her to go out and have all the fun she wants. Sex too early, however, would have prevented those powers from emerging.

Lan, Miki, and Yohko are what happens when everything goes well. Possessing power also contains an element of risk. Yukari Tatsumiya finds that out in **Doomed Megalopolis** when her brother's rape not only destroys her powers before they can develop, but leaves her abnormally subject to demonic control. Japan's psionic heroines manage to promote abstinence without denying the pleasure or power of women's sexuality.

Young American women like that. They also have a real need for such a message. According to a 1991 study by the AAUW (American Association of University Women), most American girls suffer a dramatic loss of confidence when they reach puberty. This does not seem to be a biological event. It is confined mostly to girls of European ancestry. African American and Asian American girls find their self-confidence relatively undamaged by puberty. The same is true of Japanese girls. Obviously, there are many cultural factors at work in this situation, and the media cannot be held entirely to blame. However, the absence of female, teen-aged heroes is one factor in that process. It remains to be seen if the arrival of Japanese-style heroines such as the female members of the **Mighty Morphin Power Rangers** and **Sailor Moon** on mainstream American television will have any effect on future AAUW surveys.

The gender-based powers of *anime miko* and other psionics might seem to leave men out in the cold. That's not entirely true. It is possible for men to be mediums, both in real life and in *anime*. In real life, male mediums or priests, tend to operate differently from *miko* and their secular counterparts. They tend to be more rational and more dependent on set prayers and chants, or systems such as astrology or the Chinese *Book of Changes*. They do not usually go into trances as the women do. That gives them less dramatic value, which is probably why *anime* prefers to stick with the women.

Still, male mediums do appear from time to time, although they are usually noticeably weaker than the women. For example, the official, male mediums hired by the government in ***Doomed Megalopolis*** do have some effect on whatever immediate horror is taking place, but the long-term eradication of the demonic Kato requires an intuitive female shaman like Keiko. The same is even more true of the monks in ***Zenki***. They are mostly there for comic relief, although occasionally they are allowed to hold the fort until Chiaki, her granny, and Zenki arrive to save the day.

In general, the few really effective male mediums and psionics in *anime* are quite effeminate. They are, in short, as much like women as possible. Subaru Sumeragi of ***Tokyo Babylon***, for example, is virtually indistinguishable from his twin sister except that he lacks her irritating laugh. Moreover, both he and his sister seem to be attracted to the same man, Seishirō Sakurazuka, another male medium who acts as Subaru's protector. American fans are often puzzled by Subaru and Seishirō's relationship which has both supernatural and homosexual implications that are never spelled out. That's deliberate. It creates an unspoken sensuality that underlies the entire series.

Even explicitly heterosexual male mediums like Oma Hoichiro in ***Judge*** tend to be outwardly passive if not effeminate. Oma, for example, is such a wimp at work that an explicit sex scene is necessary to establish that his relationship to Nanase is that of a lover rather than a friend. That's important because, in the end, Oma is not able to prevail entirely through his own powers. Instead, he channels through his sleeping girlfriend.

Kyōsuke of ***Kimagure Orange Road***, Soldier Blue of ***Toward the Terra***, and Roll Kran, the only male member of the psionic ***Dangaio*** team are also typically passive psychic males. So, to some degree, is Tenchi in ***Tenchi Muyō!*** He is hardly a strong character to start with, but he becomes increasingly passive as he learns that he is of alien origin and possesses unusual powers. Living in a house surrounded by love-sick demon women probably has something to do with that as well.

Even young men without powers tend to be passive in the face of female magic. Keiichi, the college freshman who falls in love with a Norse goddess in **Oh, My Goddess!,** is probably the best example of *anime*'s penchant for nerd heroes. Keiichi's relationship to Belldandy is sometimes compared to the relationship between Darren and Samantha in the American sitcom, **Bewitched**. In fact, it is precisely the reverse. Faced with the supernatural, Darren became aggressive, blustering, and sometimes downright abusive. Above all, he insisted that his wife abandon her powers so that he could remain dominant in their relationship. Keiichi makes no such demands. He makes no demands at all. He worries about what might happen if Belldandy's true nature were to be revealed, and sometimes begs her not to use her powers in public, but otherwise he revels in her ability to create an idyllic home out of a run-down temple and is grateful for her efforts. When he does intervene, it is usually because he is trying, however hopelessly, to protect her.

Nerd heroes like Tenchi, Kyōsuke, and Keiichi are the flip side of the strong, sexy female image so prevalent in *anime*. They are also a male fantasy previously unknown in the United States where nerds are played strictly for laughs. When American men want to fantasize about being irresistible to women, they must first imagine that they resemble Rambo, Superman, or possibly James Bond. Japanese men have those fantasies, too. Unfortunately, both American and Japanese men also possess mirrors. Most of them know that they lack the physical or other special powers of such superheroes. *Anime*'s nerd heroes feature more attainable attractions such as sensitivity, gentleness, and reliability. As *anime* becomes more popular, American men find that they, too, like the idea of the nerd hero. It's an appealing fantasy to imagine being completely ordinary and still able to attract beautiful, exciting women.

American women like *anime*'s nerd heroes, too. That's partly because they see them as more realistic, more indicative of what they are really likely to end up in love with. But it doesn't hurt to imagine oneself as the more exciting side of the relationship. American women are tired of Rambo. Or more accurately, they are tired of forever playing a supporting role as adoring sidekicks. *Anime* allows them to be the adored goddess for a while.

That doesn't mean that *anime* fobs women off with a promise of supernatural powers or a goddess image, while ignoring the very real problems they face because of gender. *Anime*, especially *anime* produced by female artists, often confronts women's issues directly. The issues are often the same as those raised by American feminists, and so are the complaints, but the discussion is often subtly different. *Anime* tends to stress the advantages as well as the disadvantages of being female. It does not ignore oppression, but it also recognizes that there are trade-offs.

This is certainly the case in a series like **Ranma ¹/₂**. The main character is, after all, a man who changes into a woman whenever he is splashed with cold water. That gives him an unparalleled opportunity to learn about sexual harassment and discrimination. In particular, he learns about men who cannot take no for an answer as he tries to deal with the attentions of Kuno, the self-styled high school hero, and Mikado Sanzenin, the kissing bandit of the skating rink. However, he also learns that there are some advantages to being female. Embarrassing moments like learning to skate or singing Christmas carols are easier for him in his female form, and his female persona develops a playful sense of humor. In his martial arts, too, the female Ranma learns to use speed, agility, and intelligence instead of relying too much on brute strength as he did when he was male.

Above all, Ranma finds that being a woman makes it easier for him to get to know his fiancée, Akane. At the beginning of the series, Akane is in love with Dr. Tofu who, in turn, loves her sister Kasumi. As a man, Ranma finds her situation funny in a cruel sort of way. As a woman, however, he sympathizes with her and they develop a friendship that slowly comes to affect their relationship as a couple.

Indeed, it is Ranma's support that allows Akane to make her first statement of individuality by cutting her hair short. She originally wore it long in an effort to imitate the natural femininity of her sister, Kasumi. The short hair makes her even less feminine, a touchy point with Akane who begins each school day by beating her male admirers to a bloody pulp. That's not her choice. The men have decided, without consulting Akane, that the man who defeats her in battle will be allowed to date her. Akane is proud of her martial arts training and her fighting skills, but she is also touchy about being seen as unfeminine.

That seems an unnecessary concern. Akane may be unfeminine by conventional standards, but she is easily the most popular girl in her school. She certainly has many more admirers than her conventional sister Kasumi who spends her days cooking, cleaning, and trying to find something nice to say about everything. Nice girls tend to finish last in Takahashi's works.

The contrast between pride in one's abilities and fear that an open display of such abilities will be seen as sexually undesirable is common for *anime* women. That doesn't mean that all *anime* artists see it as a valid concern. To the contrary, many *anime* directly urge young women to be true to themselves and to insist that men accept them as they are. This is certainly the case in **Silent Möbius** when Kiddy Phenil confronts the young man she loves with the fact that she is a cyborg, made of metal and considerably stronger than he is. It takes him a while to come to terms with that, but he manages.

Things don't always end so happily for strong women in *anime*. Maris, an extraterrestrial with super strength in **Supergal** finds her superpowers to be more of a curse than a blessing. To avoid smashing everything in sight with a single gesture, she wears a coiled metal harness that keeps her forever in a cramped posture and creaks painfully when she moves. As a symbol of the plight of the too-strong woman, Maris in her restraints would be hard to beat. Her strength also turns off the men. Eventually, Maris comes to the rescue of a wealthy and handsome young kidnap victim who is also the heir to a fortune. She sees this as her chance for love, money, and the good life. After a terrific battle, she leaves his kidnapper, another woman, sobbing in the dust and goes to claim her reward. Alas, men will be men even in *anime*. The young man prefers little Miss Sobbing-in-the-Dust to his rescuer.

Ogre Slayer takes on more serious women's issues such as rape. Kei Kunosuke does not downplay the danger or the trauma of rape, but she does take on an aspect of it that many American feminists might see as politically incorrect. In one episode, the anger and pain of a rape victim raises an ogre from the ground. It attacks the rapists and thus saves her. Then, however, it goes on to attack her. This is a frequent theme in **Ogre Slayer**. The anger women feel when they are attacked, harassed or discriminated against may be natural and valid, but women who let it overpower them raise an evil that will ultimately destroy them. Takahashi expresses similar concerns in her Rumik World story **The Laughing Target**, where a young woman uses hungry ghosts against two sets of would-be rapists, but in the end she becomes their tool.

Those overly concerned with political correctness are also sometimes uncomfortable with the way *anime* treats female friendships. Female bonding is important in *anime*. In fact, same-sex friendships, male and female, often seem to be much more intense than romantic relationships, at least at first. Often, however, the arrival of a romantic love interest, means the end of that friendship.

That, after all, is the whole point of **Kimagure Orange Road**. Hikaru and Madoka both falling in love with the same boy, Kyōsuke, wouldn't be much of a story if it weren't for the fact that the two girls also love each other. As a result, Madoka tries to deny her own love for Kyōsuke in order to be supportive of her more emotional and rather vulnerable friend. So far, so politically correct. The trouble is, it doesn't work. Eventually Madoka and Kyōsuke wind up in each others' arms and the friendship winds up in serious trouble. That obvious triumph of heterosexual romance over same-sex friendship strikes some American women as anti-feminist. It may well be anti-feminist but, as many young women are discovering, it often happens. Like death and other bad stuff, it needs to be faced, not denied.

At least Hikaru and Madoka's friendship remains within platonic boundaries. That's not always the case. Some of the female bonding in *anime* seems to Americans to be clearly lesbian. In **Gunbuster**, for example, the first time Noriko Takaya sees her future co-pilot, Kazumi Amano, she sees her through a haze of rose petals, the *anime* symbol of romantic infatuation if not love. Moreover, the two women's later relationship seems unusually close by American standards, and is the cause for some jealousy among other women in the series. Yet, Kazumi also loves Coach, their male drill instructor, and Noriko has a brief romance with a male cadet that clearly would have gone much further if he had lived. The **Project A-ko** series makes fun of such sentimental female attachments and jealousies, but not necessarily because they are lesbian. Male characters, too, sometimes display far greater affection toward each other than Americans are accustomed to seeing between men who are not defined as homosexuals.

All this confuses rather than shocks American *otaku*, who tend to be a fairly tolerant bunch. R.A.A., the Internet newsgroup, once spent months debating the question: "Are Japanese girls highly lesbian?" They achieved no definitive answer. That's not surprising. Their question was the wrong question. They should have asked "how do you define 'lesbian?'"

Japanese and Americans have very different definitions of what homosexuality is. Japanese accept intensely physical same-sex friendships, especially among teens, as the norm, unlike Americans who regard them as at least carrying the potential for homosexuality. Even engaging in homoerotic sexual behavior does not necessarily define a person as homosexual or lesbian. It simply describes what they are doing at that moment. This does not mean Japanese society is any more accepting of homosexual lifestyles by men or women. Japanese society is not terribly accepting of any unconventional lifestyle. There are no laws against homosexuality, but social pressure is something else, and the AIDS epidemic has brought out some very unlovely attitudes among Japanese. Still, in comparison to America, Japan is fairly tolerant.

That's partly because Japan has a long history of accepting and even idealizing same sex relationships among men. This was particularly true of the samurai. Sex was often part of the relationship between a young samurai and the man who trained him, and on the battlefield, the unswerving support of a loyal lover could mean the difference between life and death. (Jesuit priests who set up missions in Japan during the late sixteenth century were appalled by the "shameless" behavior of samurai lovers.) Off the battlefield, the entertainment quarters of Japan's feudal cities maintained numerous boy brothels.[5] They don't seem to have lacked for clients. Less is known about women, but it seems to have been accepted that women living together, such as geisha or women in polygamous marriages, were likely to sleep with each other.[6]

Japan is a bit less tolerant today. Homophobia came in along with all the other influences from the West. Like most Western influences, the degree to which homophobia has affected any particular Japanese varies. Today, Japan has no single, clearly defined attitude toward homosexuality. This, too, is reflected in *anime* where the attitude toward homosexuality depends on the individual attitude of the creator. Some *anime,* like *3 X 3 Eyes*, offer a friendly glimpse into Japan's gay life through Yakumo's friendship with Mama-san, the transvestite who owns the bar where he works. Others, like *Rei Rei,* reveal a strong anti-gay bias, although this *anime* is certainly not prudish otherwise.

Anime that deal too explicitly with gay love simply never reach the United States. That's probably just as well since they would almost certainly be misinterpreted. These are *anime* based on *bishōnen manga,* stories about gay male love which

[5]When Westerners first saw Japanese entertainment quarters they interpreted what they saw according to their own expectations. Faced with groups of all-male "entertainers" they saw a theater (Kabuki) much like that of Shakespeare's day. Faced with groups of all-female "entertainers" (geisha), they saw a red-light district. In fact, many young, attractive male "actors" never set foot on a stage, and many geisha were accomplished performers who did most of their entertaining with their clothes on.

[6]Polygamy was not very common in feudal Japan. Rich and powerful men often kept concubines, geisha, or women in a more ambiguous relationship, but usually they lived in separate residences. Only shoguns and great lords maintained actual harems.

are written for young women, and *shōjo manga* stories about lesbian romances. In fact, these stories would tell Americans little about gay life in Japan. They aren't really about gay life. The reason young Japanese women are so fascinated by same-sex relationships between men or women is because they are fascinated by the idea of equality and communication in romance.

That's very difficult to achieve in Japan today. Japan is a highly gendered society. Men and women lead very different lives. Every time they speak, their language reinforces gender differences and a patriarchal power structure. They often attend separate schools and even if they don't, boys and girls engage in very different pursuits. Later, when they marry, their lives separate again. In between, they are expected to fall in love, date, and talk to each other. Understandably, many of them find that difficult.

Most Japanese are more comfortable with their own sex. That's one of the reasons same-sex friendships are so intense. These stories about gay love are simply a means by which the gender barrier can be temporarily removed to allow for a more general discussion about the meaning and nature of romantic love. Gay men and lesbians are envied because they can find romantic love without those gender barriers.[7] They can combine love, friendship, and communication all in one wonderful package. Most Japanese women wish they could do the same. So do most Japanese men.

So do most Americans of both sexes. Unfortunately, most Americans have such strong reactions to homosexuality, positive or negative, that they may have trouble seeing these *anime* as general discussions about love. *Manga Vizion* recently published "*Love Song*," a *shōjo manga* with a lesbian theme. It will be interesting to see the response.

[7]That's only true in the fantasy world of *manga*. Real gay men and lesbians in Japan have more than enough troubles.

Possibly young Americans can get around their cultural obsession with homosexuality and see the message in these stories for what it really is. If so, the response is likely to be positive. Other *anime* which focus on the problems of communication between the sexes have done very well in the United States. **Ranma *1/2***, for example, covers the same ground in a slightly less shocking way by allowing the hero to communicate as a woman while remaining male (usually) in the romantic clinches. Young Americans, who have already noticed that men are from Mars and women from Venus in the United States as well as Japan, have made **Ranma *1/2*** one of America's best selling *anime*.

American *otaku* like the way *anime* deals with gender issues precisely because it's not the way Americans deal with them. The Japanese view of gender is not better than the American view. It's certainly not better attuned to American realities. What *anime*, does, however, is to provide a different way of looking at gender issues, one that cannot easily be defined as feminist or anti-feminist, as politically correct or politically incorrect. And that is badly needed.

Chapter Eight

Coming Full Circle

A funny thing happened on the way to the culture wars. We got run over by some cartoons. There we were, happily debating whether to focus education on multiculturalism or Western Civilization, and the kids made their own choice with *anime* and *manga*.

That's a hands-down victory for multiculturalism, but it's not necessarily a complete defeat for the West. Multiculturalism never was. The new generation that grew up on *anime* and *manga* learned at least as much about their own culture as they learned about Japan. But they did learn one thing from their early exposure to Japanese popular culture. They learned how to borrow. In addition to the increasing range of translated *anime* and *manga* on the market, American popular culture is beginning to feel the influence of these imports.

That influence is strongest in the American comic book industry, but it is also the most difficult to gauge. The rise of serious graphic novels such as Neil Gaiman's *Sandman*, Dave Sim's *Cerebus,* or Paradox Press's *Big Books*, undoubtedly owes something to *manga*, but it is also the result of long-term developments in American underground comics that have led to an increasing focus on serious topics and complex plots.

Some new comics are explicit about their debt to *manga*. In the past few years, American cartoonists have begun to create comic books featuring Japanese themes and characters, and incorporating certain stylistic elements of *manga* in the drawings. That doesn't mean Americans are being purely imitative. No true *otaku* will ever mistake these made-in-the-USA *manga* for the real article. Most true *otaku* will read them though. That's because these new American *manga* have developed into a new art form incorporating aspects of both popular cultures.

The American comic book version of *Macross II* created by James Hudnall and Schulhoff Tam, for example, bills itself as "A 100% Made-In-America Manga Original." It's not. Despite its American creators, *Macross II* is still very much a Japanese *manga*. *Macross II* is drawn in black and white, and features Japanese characters drawn in a distinctive *manga* style. The thing that really sets it apart from American comics, however, is its use of panels.

The American approach to comic book panels is straightforward. Panels are square or occasionally rectangular, and their arrangement on the page is more or less symmetrical. All action takes place within the confines of the panel. The progression of the panels from left to right across the page indicates a progression in time, usually forward. *Manga*, especially *shōjo manga*, are far more creative. Panels may take any shape, or may be absent entirely so that the action takes place in an ornate interplay that takes up a complete page. The action regularly explodes out of the panel and may intrude on another panel above, below, or to the side. The progression of panels can indicate the forward movement of time as in American comics, but can also indicate different perspectives on the same moment in time, the thought processes of a character in a single moment, or even a visual depiction of several characters' relationships to one another. Readers have to work out what each panel progression means, and in some cases, it may have more than one meaning. That style is unquestionably present in the American version of *Macross II.*

It is also present in Ben Dunn's *Ninja High School*, despite the fact that this is an original work, not a spin-off from Japanese *manga* or *anime*. Stylistically, Dunn's work is much like Japanese *manga*. That is particularly true of the black and white format and the way in which panels are used. Dunn's work also features characters drawn in the *manga* style, some common *manga* and *anime* themes such as cross dressing, and allusions to characters from other comics. However, other characters also appear, some of them more closely akin in type and appearance to the American comic book traditions, and the joking allusions to other comic book series, a common feature in Japanese *manga*, are usually to American comics such as **The Simpsons** or **Batman**.

A greater synthesis of *manga* and American comic styles is apparent in Adam Warren's *Dirty Pair*. Warren bought the rights to the *Dirty Pair* from the Japanese creator and holds more or less to the original characters and intent of the Japanese series. The two heroes are Yuri and Kei, a pair of well-built, scantily clad, intergalactic trouble-shooters. They like to style themselves as the "Lovely Angels," but the nickname they're stuck with is the "Dirty Pair." This does not refer to their clothing, sexual habits, or personal hygiene. It refers to the fact that they usually succeed in solving whatever small problem they have been assigned quite neatly, but somehow manage to create an even bigger mess in some other area. And it's never, ever their fault. In one of their Japanese adventures, for example, they used a delicate combination of brains, brawn, and pure luck to settle a difficult labor dispute on a mining planet. Unfortunately, the champagne bottle they jettisoned during their farewell celebration managed to explode the entire planet. The *Dirty Pair* was a very funny series.

And Adam Warren's version of the further adventures of Yuri and Kei is funny too. But it's also different. The American *Dirty Pair* are a bit less innocent, or perhaps just a bit less playful about their sexuality. They are drawn in a more realistic style that emphasizes their voluptuousness. In Warren's version, they look more like women and less like girls, although their behavior remains fairly unchanged. Their relationship to one another is subtly changed, however. They seem more like partners than the close friends they were in the original. This may be because they've gotten a bit older and past the age of close girlish friendships, at least according to American social conventions. As a result, their squabbling, which passed as girlish sparring in the original, sometimes sounds bitchy. The end result is neither better nor worse than the original. It is simply different.

The new comic book version of *Star Blazers* by Studio Go! (comprised of Bruce Lewis, Tim Eldred, and John Ott, with input from Steve Harrison and Albert Deschesne) features a different American-Japanese synthesis. At first, *Star Blazers* seems to be purely American. Even the American names from the original *Star Blazers* television series have been preserved. The comic is in full color and panels are more or less rectangular and progressive. However, a closer examination reveals a difference. *Star Blazers* often features panels within panels. For example, a rectangular, framed close-up of a character shooting a gun may be imposed on a larger panel showing the overall battle scene. That style is typical of *anime*. It is the way in which Japanese animators adapt the overly complex overlays of *manga* to the needs of animation. What Studio Go! has created is not based on *manga* at all. It is a comic book based on *anime*, a synthesis that is, in itself, a new creation.

The same is true of the content of *Star Blazers*. Studio Go!'s attention to detail and consistency, and the care they take to fit their stories into the overall Yamato series is very American. Japanese cartoonists have no objection to writing several different, contradictory versions of the same story or placing well established characters in a completely different story line without explaining how they got there. Japanese fans accept this, but it troubles Americans. Indeed, the first volume of the American *Star Blazers* comic book included a short essay explaining how and why the feature film, **Farewell to Space Battleship Yamato,** seemed to be a different version of the television series that aired as the second season of **Star Blazers**. In fact, the series was an expanded version of the movie with a different, happier ending. There's nothing Studio Go! can do about such inconsistencies in the originals, but they do take care that their own additions do not add to the confusion. Their additions are carefully fitted into gaps in the original, or may retell a story from a different perspective. The first approach is distinctively American, the second owes more to Japanese influences.

Not all American comics with Japanese themes are necessarily influenced by *manga* or *anime*. William Tucci's *Shi: The Way of the Warrior*, for example, may owe something to Japanese gangster (*yakuza*) movies, but its content and style is clearly American. The series is realistically drawn in full color, and shows an attention to detail that is unknown in *manga*, although Tucci occasionally makes use of older Japanese styles drawn from woodblock prints or warrior scrolls. The content, too, is definitely American despite the inclusion of Japanese characters, philosophy, and customs. Tucci begins his stories with the same types of mysteries and seemingly insoluble dilemmas that Japanese cartoonists love, but he is too American to leave them unclarified and resolved. Although *Shi* makes direct references to Japanese history and to present day Japan, it is essentially an American view of Japan and little influenced by Japanese culture.

The opposite is true of *Usagi Yojimbo*, created by Stan Sakai. At first glance, Sakai's style seems very mainstream American with its cutely anthropomorphic animals and neatly framed, progressive panels. In fact, Sakai has carried that style to its logical extreme. Stylistically, *Usagi Yojimbo* owes nothing to *manga* or *anime*. Instead, it shows what can be done within the confines of American comic book conventions.

The content of *Usagi Yojimbo*, however, does owe something to *anime* and *manga* influences. That's not just because the characters and themes are Japanese. Actually, *Usagi Yojimbo* makes no direct claim to historical Japan at all. Its hero, Miyamoto Usagi, inhabits an alternate universe which just happens to resemble high feudal (*sengoku*) Japan in all respects except that the lead characters are animals.[1] Usagi is a *ronin*, a masterless samurai. He dresses appropriately in *haori* (top coat) and *hakama* (divided trousers), wears his ears in a formal topknot, and carries two swords. The series is peppered with references to Japanese religion, customs and food, sometimes with explanation, but often not. In one episode, Usagi meets a burned out soldier who describes himself as an *ashigaru*. A caption explains that an *ashigaru* is a peasant foot soldier or infantryman. On the other hand, when Usagi feeds his rice balls to a bunch of hungry lizards, there is no caption to explain that these white triangles with a black strip represent rice pressed into triangular form and wrapped with a strip of *nori* (black seaweed). It is as if Sakai is deliberately introducing some of the confusion that occurs naturally in Japanese works as a result of cultural differences. This suggests that confusion may be part of the attraction of *anime* and *manga*. The confusion itself is part of what makes it such a satisfying fantasy.[2]

Sakai is obviously aware of other reasons for the popularity of *anime* and *manga*. In particular, he introduces themes of loss, loneliness, and death in this deceptively childlike comic. *Usagi Yojimbo* has much the same feel to it as Leiji Matsumoto's classic *anime* **Galaxy Express 999** and

[1] Usagi's name alone could use some explanation. He introduces himself as "Miyamoto Usagi" using the Japanese name order. Some fans may realize this; others will assume that his first name is Miyamoto. Some fans will also know that "usagi" is the Japanese word for "rabbit," and some will realize the use of "Miyamoto" as a family name is an allusion to "Musashi" Miyamoto, the samurai who wrote **The Five Rings**.

[2] On the other hand, the original confusion may have been excessive. Sakai has now begun to include historical notes, a fine thing for students of Japanese history, since his re-creation of this era is extraordinarily detailed and exact.

Arcadia of My Youth, except that the two have been combined. The series alternates between stories of Usagi as an adult rabbit and flashbacks to his training back in the years before he tied his ears in a topknot.[3] Like Tetsuo in ***Galaxy Express 999,*** the young Usagi is trusting and idealistic. He is overly prone to accept people and the world at their own evaluation. He has one advantage over ***Galaxy Express 999***'s Tetsuo. Sakai has given him a more reliable mentor, a wise and experienced martial arts master instead of a mysterious and unpredictable woman like Maytel. As an American, Sakai couldn't quite bring himself to create a completely amoral universe, but he comes close.

The world of the adult Usagi is less kind. His master worked hard to teach his young pupil to be cautious but not cynical, honorable but not foolish, and gentle but not weak. He succeeded. The adult Usagi is a bit rough and ready in his ways, but he's a softy underneath, always ready to help the down and out. That won't necessarily save him. It certainly doesn't save those he meets on the way, many of whom meet the sudden, pointless, undeserved ends typical of *anime* and *manga.* And it doesn't save Usagi from a life of sadness and loss. He is a *ronin* and nothing in his life is permanent. Friends die or move on. Even if they do neither, Usagi moves on. His character is reminiscent of Captain Harlock in ***Arcadia of My Youth***, if you can imagine Harlock with rabbit ears.

The influence of *anime* on American animation is not yet as evident except, perhaps, for the unfortunate differences between Disney Studios and Tezuka Productions over ***The Lion King.*** That's partly because most American animation remains wedded to children's entertainment, while most *anime* imports are geared to an adult audience.[4] ***Heavy Metal*** and Peter Chung's ***Aeon Flux***, which aired on MTV, are so far the closest America has come to mainstream adult animation.[5] They do show some signs of *anime*'s influence stylistically as well as in the amoral, unresolved plots and the ambiguous relationships of the characters. So far, however, ***Heavy Metal*** and ***Aeon Flux*** stand alone.

That's likely to change as more *anime* makes its way onto mainstream American television. The two latest offerings, ***Sailor Moon***, a magical girl series, and ***Dragon Ball***, a little boy on a quest series, have gone down well. Others seem likely to follow.

[3]This is a visual allusion that could use some explanation. Young men of the samurai class wore their hair loose. Only when they became men did they shave their foreheads and tie the remaining hair in a topknot.

[4]In fact, Japanese animators produce some delightful things for children, but few are imported to America, probably because that ground is already fully covered. Two exceptions to this rule are ***My Neighbor Totoro*** and ***Night on the Galactic Railroad.***

[5]American animators do produce adult-oriented features, some of them excellent. But they are unsung heroes in their own land, and performances are usually limited to art shows and animation festivals. Most Americans never see their work.

Some influence is already noticeable. The animated version of **Batman** grows darker and more adult by the minute. Other superhero shows like **The X-Men, Exosquad, Wild C.A.T.S.,** and **The Savage Dragon**, although still essentially dominated by muscles and action, have begun to feature somewhat darker themes and stronger roles for an increasing number of women. Characters are a bit more developed and their relationships with one another a bit more complex.

But American television has its limits. A recent **Exosquad** episode introduced a plot that could have been drawn directly from *anime*. Maul, a good-hearted but repulsively muscular mutant with horns growing out of his back, confided his deepest secret to his comrades. Fearing rejection, he had never told his father about his mutation. He had simply left home leaving his father to wonder if he was dead or alive. In the subsequent episode, Maul and his father meet.

In the world of *anime*, this could play out many ways. Maul might never even identify himself to the old man who would go on his way tragically and ironically unaware of the fact that he had found his son. Or Maul could identify himself only to be rejected exactly as he had feared. Or there might be a touching reunion between father and son followed by the sad realization that Maul's mutation precludes any normal family life and a heart-breaking farewell. American television isn't ready for any of those. Instead, Maul identifies himself to his father, saves the old boy's life and an emotional reunion ensues. Maul promises to stay in touch and visit more often. That ending could also be an option in *anime*. The Japanese are not averse to a bit of schmaltz now and then. The problem with the **Exosquad** ending is not that it wasn't an option, but that it was the only option and the audience knew it.

The same is true of other American cartoons like **Gargoyles, Teen-Age Mutant Ninja Turtles,** or even **Duckman**. These reveal some of the ambiguities that delight fans of *anime*, but are less satisfying in the end. Although their characters may be odd and sometimes perversely flawed, in the end it's clear who the good guys and the bad guys are. That strict division is probably more at the insistence of sponsors and television executives than cartoonists, but for as long as it continues, American animation is doomed to remain in the kiddie corner.

Those strictures may annoy American *otaku*, but they often delight the Japanese. After all, Americans find *anime* and *manga* fascinating because they're alien. The stories may be old hat to the Japanese, but we haven't heard them yet. The Japanese feel the same way. They haven't heard our myths yet either. Moreover, American cartoons and comics are as revealing of American culture as *manga* and *anime* are of Japanese culture. As the alien concepts revealed in *anime* and *manga* force Americans to reexamine some of their most basic assumptions, American popular culture forces the Japanese to take another look at themselves.

Although Disney movies have long been popular in Japan, American superheroes and other animated works were relatively unknown until recently. In April 1994, **The X-Men** made their first appearance on Japanese TV. The comic books and related merchandise followed soon after. The event did not leave *anime* and *manga* creators trembling in their boots. **The X-Men** were not an overnight sensation. Most Japanese continued to prefer their native product. *Amecomi* (American comics) did, however, draw a small dedicated following, much as *anime* and *manga* did when they first arrived in America. Their influence on *anime* is not yet apparent, but it's coming. Already, a Japanese-drawn version of **Spiderman** teaches English on educational TV.

We have come full circle. *Amecomi* fans in Japan are the mirror images of American *otaku*. Like American *otaku*, they struggle to understand the cultural subcontext of what is going on. They attend their conventions, dress as their favorite characters, and show a missionary-like zeal in attempting to introduce their friends to the delights of American animation and comics. They fret about the difficulty of ever producing a perfect translation, one that conveys the feeling as well as the meaning of the English original.

Despite the concerns of American *otaku* and Japanese *amecomi* fans, the meanings are getting through. At least, they're getting through better than they ever have before. Trading comic books and cartoons may not be what educators had in mind when they argued in favor of multiculturalism. But it's a beginning and it's not a bad beginning at that.

Appendix A

How to Become an Otaku

Becoming an *otaku* is easy. First, if you're lurking in the back of the bookstore reading this, march up to the register and buy this book. Then, watch as many *anime* as you can find. As all *otaku* know, that's not always as easy as it sounds. *Anime* has become increasingly available in the past few years. It's no longer necessary to attend Star Trek conferences in the hope of trading fan-subbed copies with other *otaku*. National chains like Blockbuster Video have inaugurated a separate "animation" section which consists primarily of (mostly dubbed) Japanese animation. Video outlets specializing in foreign films have also discovered *anime*. And mail order *anime* catalogues have proliferated.

Americans living in cities have an easier time becoming *otaku*, especially if they live in New York or anywhere on the west coast. That's because there are a lot of Japanese living in these areas:

students, artists, business types, and other assorted ex-patriots. Their presence has long since led to the creation of Japan-related neighborhoods like San Francisco's "Nihonmachi," L.A.'s "Little Tokyo," or Seattle's more generic "International District." Simply wandering through such neighborhoods will quickly acquaint *otaku* wanna-be's with the full range of *anime* paraphernalia. It may also result in friendships with overseas Japanese willing to share their enthusiasm for *anime* and *manga*, and provide much needed commentary on both.

The first discovery will probably be the video rental clubs. Most of these charge a small membership fee (ten or twenty dollars as a rule), but they're well worth it since they carry a much wider range of *anime* than is available anywhere else. They also carry a lot of live-action films. It's a good idea to check the shelves carefully before joining. Some clubs carry only Japanese language materials. Most, however, prefer to stock subtitled versions whenever possible, because these appeal equally to English and Japanese speaking audiences.

They also carry some *anime* without any English translation that simply aren't otherwise available in the United States. Some of these are sufficiently visual that even the Japanese-impaired can understand what's going on. There are also a variety of home pages on the Internet that include scripts or at least synopses of as yet untranslated *anime*. The best way to deal with a Japanese-only *anime* is to watch it with a Japanese friend who can translate and explain.

That's not difficult to do. Many overseas Japanese find life in America lonely and confusing. Most of them do speak some English, but worry (sometimes with cause) that Americans will laugh at their efforts. They are eager to make friends, and many friendships develop naturally from conversations begun at video clubs. For those who are not so outgoing, there are other alternatives. The easiest is to answer one of the many ads asking to exchange Japanese lessons for English conversation practice. The best place to look for such ads is on the bulletin boards maintained by many shops in Japanese neighborhoods. Video clubs often have them; Japanese supermarkets always do. If there is a local English newspaper catering to the Asian American community, that's also a good place to look. Some Americans are put off by the fear that the person who placed the ad is actually looking for a sex partner or an experienced English teacher. That is rarely the case.

In addition to the video clubs, Japanese ethnic neighborhoods feature a number of other stores that carry merchandise of interest to the *otaku*. Bookstores, for example, often stock *manga* in both English translation and Japanese. The largest bookstore to look out for is

Kinokuniya. Kinokuniya is one of Japan's largest chain bookstores, and it now has branches in most major American cities. For the most part, Kinokuniya caters to a Japanese clientele, but they do include an English language section containing books about Japan and translations of Japanese works including many *manga*. Would-be *otaku* should also check out the Japanese language *manga* section at Kinokuniya for an idea of how much there is to choose from. Kinokuniya has branches in the following locations:

665 Paularino Dr.
Costa Mesa, CA 92626
(714) 434-9986

595 River Road
Edgewater, NJ
(201) 941-7580

Japan Center
1581 Webster St.
San Francisco, CA 94115
(415) 567-7625

10 West 49th St.
New York, NY
(212) 745-1461

675 Saratoga Ave.
San Jose, CA 95129
(408) 252-1300

519 Sixth St. South
Seattle, WA
(206) 587-2477

123 South Onizuki St.
Suite 205
Los Angeles, CA 90012
(213) 687-4447

In addition, toy stores in Japanese ethnic neighborhoods frequently carry *anime* related dolls, kits, posters, and other fun stuff. Music stores often stock *anime* sound tracks.

It's harder for someone who lives in a city without such a district or in a rural area to become an *otaku*, but it's no longer impossible. It just requires a bit more creativity. In the absence of a separate district, the best place to start looking for *anime* is probably the phone book. Outlets that specialize in foreign films are likely to carry some *anime*, so are larger chain outlets. Blockbuster is a very good place to start for rentals. Sam Goody and SunCoast Video offer a lot of *anime* for sale, and are often located in smaller towns. Comic book stores are also a good place to look. Most do carry some *manga*, and many also carry *anime* or will at least order them.

Another good place to call is the local college if there is one. Many colleges have an *anime* club. At the very least, this means that they meet regularly to share their films. Some clubs also maintain rental libraries.

Eventually, however, *otaku* living inland or in rural areas realize the grim truth. They are going to have to spend more money on *anime* than they would if they lived elsewhere. Fortunately, *anime, manga* and related paraphernalia are available through mail order catalogues. Many distributors include a phone number on their videos for anyone wishing to order from them. *The Complete Anime Guide: Japanese Animation Video Directory & Resource Guide* by Trish Ledoux and Doug Ranney gives a full listing of how to reach individual distributors. Those willing to sell their products directly through mail order catalogues are:

A.D. Vision
Southwest Plaza Bldg.
5750 Bintliff, #217
Houston, TX 77036-2123
(713) 977-9181 (phone)
(713) 977-5573 (fax)

AnimEigo, Inc.
P.O. Box 989
Wilmington, NC 28402-0989
(910) 251-1850 (phone)
(910) 763-2376 (fax)
questions@animeigo.com
http://www.animeigo.com

Software Sculptors
149 Madison Ave, Suite 202
New York, NY 10016
(212) 679-1171 (phone)
(212) 679-2322 (fax)

U.S. Renditions
1123 Dominguez St, Suite K
Carson, CA 90746
(310) 604-9701 (phone)
(310) 604-1134 (fax)

Voyager Entertainment, Inc.
456 Sylvan Ave.
Englewood Cliffs, NJ 07632
(800) 704-4040 (phone)
(201) 569-2998 (fax)

However, not all distributors offer retail services and ordering *anime* separately from individual companies takes a lot of time and usually raises the shipping and handling costs. In general, it's best to order as much as possible from one source. The following mail order companies feature informative catalogues, reasonable prices, reliable service, and carry a wide range of merchandise in addition to their own products:

The Right Stuf
P.O. Box 71309
Des Moines, IA 50325-1309
(800) 338-6827 (phone)
(515) 279-7434 (fax)
atomu@centsys.com

Viz Shop By Mail
P.O. Box 77010
San Francisco, CA 94107
(800) 394-3042 (phone)
(415) 546-7086 (fax)
http://www.viz.com

Central Park Media
250 W. 57th St., Suite 317
New York, NY 10107
Phone: (800) 626-4277
FAX: (212) 977-8709

Once you get on their mailing list, most of these companies will send you updated catalogues. However, the best way to keep up with what's going on and, perhaps more important, what's coming out next, is to subscribe to *Animerica*, a monthly magazine devoted exclusively to *anime*. Fans sometimes complain that *Animerica* is overly commercial and contains too many ads. If, however, your aim is to find out what's available with English translations, ads are not necessarily a bad thing. For more in depth analyses, *Anime FX*, a British publication is available through an American distributor. In addition, *Animation Magazine*, the American animation industry's trade journal, usually contains at least one article on *anime*. Fans of *manga* will probably also want to subscribe to *Manga Vizion*, a monthly publication featuring translated *manga* in the serialized style of Japanese monthlies. Those who are studying Japanese, might also be interested in *Mangajin*, a rather more scholarly publication which uses *manga* as a way to discuss colloquial Japanese language and Japanese culture in general. To subscribe, contact these companies directly at:

Animation Magazine
28024 Dorothy Dr., Suite 200
Agoura Hills, CA 91301
(800) 996-8666 (phone)
(818) 991-3773

Anime FX
Heritage Press
3150 State Line Rd.
North Bend, OH 45052

Animerica
P.O. Box 77010
San Francisco, CA 94107
(415) 546-7073, ext. 27
http://www.viz.com
viz@netcom.com

Manga Vizion
P.O. Box 77010
San Francisco, CA 94107
(415) 546-7073, ext. 27
http://www.viz.com
viz@netcom.com

Mangajin
P.O. Box 7119
Marietta, GA 30065

The following magazines will also be of interest to aspiring *okatu:*

Animeco
c/o Limelight Publishing
1513 Young St., Suite 202
Honolulu, HI 96826
whols@aloha.net
http://planet-hawaii.com/
    lime/anim.html

V.Max
P.O. Box 3292
Santa Clara, CA 95055
(510) 549-1726 (fax)
mrwarmth@vmax.com

Protoculture Addicts
P.O. Box 1433, Sation "B"
Montreal, Qc.
CANADA H3B 3L2
(514) 527-0347 (fax)
flip@odyssee.net
http://www.odyssee.net/-flip/PA

Another good way to keep up and keep in touch is to attend one or more of the many *anime* conventions which are held each year. Conventions vary a lot, but most feature previews of upcoming releases, some Japanese animation that may or may not appear in English translation, dealer displays, panel discussions, and guests of honor. Conventions provide a superb opportunity to sample *anime* you might like to buy and to see some that may never actually make it to the American market. The guests of honor often include Japanese animators and voice actors you are unlikely to meet anywhere else. Don't worry about the costume competitions. Some fans like to go dressed as their favorite characters, but if you're feeling shy, there's no rule that says you have to. Most conventions are held at roughly the same time and place each year, but exact dates and locales vary. The following conventions are listed by season. More specific information can be obtained by contacting the relevant organizations at the addresses, phone numbers, and e-mail addresses below.

Summer

Anime America: Bay Area, CA
333 Cobalt Way, Suite 107
Sunnyvale, CA 94086
anam@rahul.net

Anime Expo: L.A., CA
2425 B Channing, Suite 684
Berkeley, CA 94704
shogun@sutro.sfsu.edu

Project A-Kon: Dallas, TX
810 Blossom Rd.
Garland, TX 75041
(214) 278-6935 (fax)
phoenix@pic.net

Autumn

Anime Weekend: Atlanta, GA
P.O. Box 13544
Atlanta, GA 30324-0544
(404) 364-9773 (phone)
awaadmin@peach.america.net

Otakon: State College, PA
Dave Asher
661A Waupelani Dr.
State College, PA 16801
(814) 867-3478 (phone)
dcasher@delphi.com

Winter

Anime East: NJ
Atlantic Anime Alliance
P.O. Box 10371
New Brunswick, NJ 08906-0371
(908) 719-9770
anime.east@genie.com

Fanime Con: CA
P.O. Box 642028
San Jose, CA 95164-2028
abunai@ibm.net

KatsuCon: VA
Katsu Productions, Ltd.
P.O. Box 11582
Blacksburg, VA 24062-1582
katsucon@vtserf.cc.vt.edu

Project Z-Kon: TX
P.O. Box 450004
Garland, TX 75045-000

The final stage of becoming an *otaku* involves going to Japan. For that, contact your travel agent and don't forget to bring your frog.[1]

[1] A Japanese travel charm takes the form of a small, green frog called a "buji ni kaeru." This is an elaborate pun which can mean either "safety frog" or "come-back safely." Those who knew that are probably already full-fledged otaku.

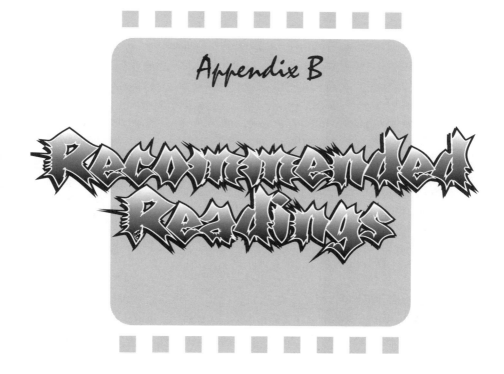

Appendix B

Recommended Readings

On Anime and Manga:

Trish Ledoux and Doug Ranney. *The Complete Anime Guide: Japanese Animation Video Directory & Resource Guide.* Tiger Mountain Press, 1995.

> *It's exactly what it says it is, a very complete guide to what's available in America and how to get your hands on it. The opening chapter on the history of anime in America is excellent. One major weakness in the Video Directory itself is that the synopses are heavily based on materials provided by the distributors. This doesn't make them bad, but a bit more critical commentary would be useful. This book is a must for any aspiring otaku.*

Frederik L. Schodt. *Dreamland Japan: Writings on Manga.* Stone Bridge Press, 1996

> Dreamland Japan *is more than just an updated version of Manga! Manga!. It's a whole different book, a collection of essays on various aspects of Japan's comic book industry including a discussion of the social debate about manga's impact on Japanese youth, a whole chapter on the life and legacy of Osamu Tezuka, and a truly wonderful collection of thumbnail sketches of the unconventional lifestyles of many of Japan's leading cartoonists. Anime fans may be a bit disappointed that the book touches on animation only briefly, but much of what Schodt has to say about manga applies equally well to amine.*

Frederik L. Schodt. *Manga! Manga!: The World of Japanese Comics.* Kodansha International, 1983.

> *An excellent discussion of the manga world and its audience. Most of the examples and facts are out of date by now, but the book isn't, which is a testament to how good it was in the first place. It doesn't say much about anime both because of when it was written and because the author's interests were elsewhere. Mr. Schodt has now produced an updated discussion of manga, but this earlier work is still worth a look.*

Kevin Quigley, Editor, *Comics Underground Japan,* Blast Books, 1996.

> *How do you define "underground" comics in a country where risqué comics for adults are mainstream?* Comics Underground Japan *offers only a few answers in its regrettably short introduction, but it provides a wealth of examples in the form of translated excerpts from* Garo, *an offbeat and decidedly non-mainstream manga monthly. Titles include "Mary's Asshole," "Planet of the Jap," and "Cat Noodle Soup." None of these excerpts are likely to be animated soon, but they're definitely worth a read.*

Scott McCloud. *Understanding Comics: An Invisible Art,* Kitchen Sink Press, Inc., 1993.

> *Everything you already knew about comics but never put into words, and lot you didn't know. Written as a comic, the cartoonist takes you*

through the history of comics and the visual tricks you follow so easily and never notice. McCloud includes only two short sections on manga. The rest is about American comics, but it's still worth reading.

On Japanese Contemporary Culture:

Matt Taro Greenfeld. *Speed Tribes,* HarperCollins Publishers, 1994.

A well written book about what it's like to be young and Japanese in the 1990s. Each chapter describes a life story. It's a bit short on women's lives, and tends to focus on the sensational. It doesn't say anything about anime, but it says a lot about the people anime was originally created for.

Ian Buruma. *Behind the Mask: On Sexual Demons, Sacred Mothers, Transvestites, Gangsters, and Other Japanese Cultural Heroes.* Pantheon Books, 1985.

A discussion of Japanese popular culture based primarily on media imagery. Sadly, it doesn't say much about anime, but it does talk about manga and a lot of the analyses of live-action movies apply equally well to anime.

Nicholas Bornoff. *Pink Samurai: Love, Marriage & Sex in Contemporary Japan,* Pocket Books, 1991.

It's exactly what the title says it is, except that there isn't as much on love and marriage as there is on sex. The book rambles a bit and tends toward the sensational, but then so does anime. This may at least give otaku some idea of the sexual references in anime.

Sumiko Iwao. *The Japanese Woman: Traditional Image and Changing Reality,* Harvard University Press, 1993.

A generational study of the changing roles and expectations of Japanese women. It doesn't say anything about anime or manga, but it does give a good picture of some of the rapid changes the media portray. It's a bit overly optimistic, but essentially accurate and up-to-date. It's also a bit on the scholarly side, but understandable even for readers without any background in Japanese culture.

Appendix B

On Japanese History:

Ivan Morris. *The Nobility of Failure: Tragic Heroes in the History of Japan*, Meridian Books, 1975.

> *Morris addresses the same question that plagues many otaku: why do the Japanese like heroes who die and/or lose? It didn't begin with anime. In this book, Morris introduces the original stories of tragic heroes from Japan's earliest history to World War II. Otaku will recognize some of the names; they will certainly recognize the themes.*

Chieko Irie Mulhern, Ed. *Heroic With Grace: Legendary Women of Japan*, M. E. Sharpe, Inc., 1991.

> *Because Morris wrote in the 1970s, it didn't occur to him to include any female heroes in his collection although there were plenty to choose from. This book attempts to redress the balance. It's a more scholarly work and not always suitable for someone without a background in Japanese history. It's also a collection of essays so the quality varies quite a bit.*

Charles A. Dunn. *Everyday Life in Traditional Japan*, Charles E. Tuttle Company, 1983.

> *An overview of what life was like for different classes in Tokugawa era (1601–1868) Japan. It's written for the layreader, nicely illustrated with black and white renditions of woodblock prints, and very useful for anyone who enjoys historical anime.*

John Green. *Life in Old Japan Coloring Book*, Dover Publications, Inc., 1994.

> *An even easier introduction to the look and feel of Tokugawa Japan. It's not really as childish as it looks. It does contain a reasonable amount of accurate information, but don't forget to bring your crayons!*

On Japanese Religion and Folklore:

Ian Reader. *Religion in Contemporary Japan*, University of Hawaii Press, 1991.

A clearly written overview of the syncretic mix of religions in Japan today. Reader's study is particularly good in that it discusses practice as well as doctrine.

Carmen Blacker. *The Catalpa Bow: A Study of Shamanistic Practices in Japan*, Unwin Hyman, Ltd., 1986.

A rather scholarly study that assumes some prior knowledge about Japan, but it's well written and anyone who perseveres will be able to get the gist. A must for anyone with a taste for supernatural anime who wants to know how much of that stuff is real. How much? More than you think.

Helen and William McAlpine. *Japanese Tales and Legends.* Oxford University Press, 1979.

A well written and charmingly illustrated collection of some of Japan's more popular myths and folk stories. The first two sections are readable retelling of some of the Shinto myths related in the Nihongi and the Kojiki. This is certainly easier than reading the awkward translations of the originals that are available. Unfortunately, the selection is a bit random so the whole doesn't hang together as well as it might.

Mirium Cox and Kingo Fujii. *The Three Treasures: Myths of Old Japan.* Harper & Row, 1964.

A beautifully illustrated and more complete retelling of the myths contained in the Nihongi and Kojiki. It also contains a number of popular folk tales. Unfortunately, it's out of print, but it is available in many libraries.

Juliet Piggott. *Japanese Mythology,* Peter Bedrick Books, 1969.

A nicely illustrated, well organized introduction to some of the basic myths and legends. Despite the title, it's not confined to mythology. It also includes a fair number of warrior legends and other folklore. It's also out of print. Try the library.

E. Dale Saunders. *Mudra: A Study of the Symbolic Gestures in Japanese Buddhist Sculpture,* Princeton University Press, 1985.

Appendix B

A lot more than the average otaku probably wants to know about Japanese Buddhism, but the illustrations include much of the Buddhist paraphernalia (such as the ubiquitous "vajra") that appear regularly in anime along with the name of each and a brief explanation of what it is.

Appendix C

A Glossary of Anime Terms

amecomi: Japanese slang meaning American comics.

anime: Japanese animation films.

bishōnen: The literal meaning is "beautiful boy." *Bishōnen manga* are stories about beautiful young men in love with each other. They are not produced for a gay audience but for young women. *Bishōnen* is also sometimes used as an adjective for any young man who is portrayed as more beautiful than handsome. CLAMP, for example, uses a *bishonen* style.

bosozoku: The literal meaning is "speed tribes." Actually, it refers to motorcycle gangs.

Bunraku: Japan's puppet theater. Bunraku developed at the same time as Kabuki and uses many of the same scripts. However, the use of puppets adds an element of artificiality that is continued today in the form of *anime*.

CLAMP: A four-woman group based in Osaka which produces a large number of popular *manga* and *anime* featuring exceptionally beautiful and sexually ambiguous young men in eerie, gothic settings.

dōshin: The police of the Tokugawa era (1601–1868). See *jitte*.

etchi: The Japanese pronunciation of the English letter "H." The "H" stands for *hentai* which means strange or, more commonly, sexually perverted.

fan-subs: Subtitled *anime* created by unauthorized fans who edit their own translations onto a Japanese tape. Copies are usually distributed free and some fan-subbers feel this makes what they do all right. Morally speaking, that may be true, but legally they are still in violation of copyright laws.

furigana: *Hiragana* (and occasionally *katakana*) written beside *kanji* to show the correct pronunciation. These often appear in *manga* to aid children or the less literate (like native English speakers!). They may also be used when a *kanji* has been given an unusual pronunciation.

giri: A feudal concept of duty or obligation. See *ninjo*.

hakama: Floor length wide trousers usually worn by men although *miko* also wear them as part of their religious regalia.

hentai: See *etchi*.

hiragana: A Japanese syllabary used to add verb endings, or for Japanese words not written with *kanji*.

jitte: A steel rod with a hook used by police in the Tokugawa era (1601–1868) to disarm samurai with swords. They also make an appearance in **Cyber City Oedo 808**, but there, too, the reference is to Tokugawa Japan.

Kabuki: An all-male theatrical tradition in which female impersonators play the women's roles. Kabuki often plays off of this by having characters masquerade as the opposite sex, whatever that is. This tradition has obviously also found its way into *anime*. Kabuki staging techniques and sound effects have also influenced *anime*.

kami: Usually translated as a Shinto god, but the reference really means something more like spirit or soul.

kanji: Ideographic characters borrowed from China and used to write Japanese.

katakana: A Japanese syllabary mostly used to write foreign words. When foreigners appear in *manga*, their words are often written in *katakana*.

kōhai: An underclassman or junior student in a relationship. See *sempai*.

manga: Japanese comic books or graphic novels. They begin as serialized entries in monthly magazines. If they are popular, they are collected into books or series of books. Most *anime* are based on popular *manga*.

mecha: A *katakana* word derived from the English word "mechanical." In *anime* it can refer to any kind of machine, but usually is applied to robots and other large, high tech items.

miko: A Shinto priestess. *Miko* usually wear red *hakama* with a white top, although they sometimes also appear dressed completely in white.

mono no aware: The aesthetic theory that true beauty is increased by an awareness of transience. A flower, for example, is all the more beautiful because we know it will soon wither and die. As a result, all deep beauty is also sad.

ninja: A mercenary spy or assassin in feudal Japan. The *ninja* were trained in special techniques known as *ninjutsu* and were often thought to have supernatural abilities.

ninjō: Human feelings or personal inclinations, usually used when they are in opposition to duty. See *giri*.

Noh: Japan's ancient classical theater. It is known for its slow, deliberate movements, its somber, supernatural plots, and its eerie chanting and sound effects. Noh has influenced every aspect of Japanese entertainment including *anime*.

otaku: An *anime* fan. The term literally means "you" in a very formal sense. In Japan, it has come to mean people who are obsessed with something to the point where they have few close personal relationships. The nature of the obsession can be anything from *anime* to computers. In Japan *otaku* has the same negative connotations as "nerd." In America, however, it refers specifically to *anime* fans. Whether or not it has negative connotations depends on the context and the tone of voice.

OAV: See OVA.

OVA: An acronym for "Original Video Animation." This means that it's part of a series but was never actually aired on TV. Often these are series that began on television, but some begin life as OVAs. Some *otaku* and distributors prefer to use OAV for "Original Animated Video."

r.a.a.: Until recently, the abbreviation for rec.arts.anime, the Internet newsgroup for *anime* fans. Due to sheer volume, it was broken up into nine categories including rec.arts.anime.creative, rec.arts.-anime.fandom, rec.arts.anime.games, rec.arts.anime.info, rec.arts.-anime.marketplace, rec.arts.anime.models, rec.arts.anime.music, and rec.arts.manga. The fan discussions that were the mainstay of the old r.a.a. are now continued on rec.arts.anime.misc.

samurai: Japan's warrior caste. It does not refer exclusively to a man in armor, but covers the whole class. There are female samurai (some of them even fight) and even little, bitty baby samurai.

sempai: Translating this as upperclassman doesn't really get the meaning across. The relationship of a senior student to his/her junior carries a much larger number of privileges and responsibilities in Japan than it does in the U.S. Moreover, the relationship between a *sempai* and his/her *kōhai* (underclassman) lasts the rest of their lives. See *kōhai*.

seppuku: Ritual suicide by disembowelment. This is sometimes also called *harakiri*, but that term implies disapproval.

Shinto: Japan's indigenous religion. Literally it means "the way of the gods." Shinto contains over 8 million gods or *kami*, and even more stories. A lot of *anime* is based on Shinto mythology and folklore.

shōjo: A young girl. *Shōjo manga* refers specifically to *manga* written for girls or women. Japanese differentiate between *shōjo* (girls') *manga* and *redisu* (ladies') but American *otaku* tend to call them all *shōjo*. Often *shōjo* is also used as an adjective to describe *anime* that is not specifically for women but emphasizes emotions and personal relationships.

shōnen: A young boy. *Shōnen manga* refers specifically to *manga* written for boys or men. Japanese differentiate between *shōnen* (boys') *manga, seinen* (young men's) *manga,* and *seijin* (adult) *manga* but American *otaku* tend to call them all *shōnen.* Often *shōnen* is also used as an adjective to describe *anime* that is not specifically for men but emphasizes action.

super-deformed: A way of drawing *anime* characters so that they appear as cute, toddler-like versions of themselves. Superdeformed characters often appear in the opening or closing credits. This style is also sometimes used to highlight comic moments or as a form of satire.

Takarazuka: An all-female theater troup in which male impersonators play the male roles. The Takarazuka theater is very popular with teen-aged girls and has had a big influence on *shōjo ßmanga.* Some of the characteristics of many *anime* male characters are more clearly explainable if you realize that the artist may be drawing a woman playing a man.

Interior and cover design by Todd Sanders. Headline font created by Scott Player. Typesetting by The Publishing Services Group, Princeton, Illinois.